CW00685853

Historical Linguistics

Herbert Schendl is Professor of English
Linguistics at the University of Vienna

Series Editor H.G. Widdowson

Historical Linguistics

Herbert Schendl

OXFORD
UNIVERSITY PRESS

OXFORD
UNIVERSITY PRESS

Great Clarendon Street, Oxford OX2 6DP

Oxford University Press is a department of the University of Oxford.
It furthers the University's objective of excellence in research, scholarship,
and education by publishing worldwide in

Oxford New York

Auckland Cape Town Dar es Salaam Hong Kong Karachi
Kuala Lumpur Madrid Melbourne Mexico City Nairobi
New Delhi Shanghai Taipei Toronto

With offices in

Argentina Austria Brazil Chile Czech Republic France Greece
Guatemala Hungary Italy Japan Poland Portugal Singapore
South Korea Switzerland Thailand Turkey Ukraine Vietnam

OXFORD and OXFORD ENGLISH are registered trade marks of
Oxford University Press in the UK and in certain other countries

ISBN-13: 978 0 19 437238 1

Printed in China

Contents

Preface

Purpose

What justification might there be for a series of introductions to language study? After all, linguistics is already well served with introductory texts: expositions and explanations which are comprehensive, authoritative, and excellent in their way. Generally speaking, however, their way is the essentially academic one of providing a detailed initiation into the discipline of linguistics, and they tend to be lengthy and technical: appropriately so, given their purpose. But they can be quite daunting to the novice. There is also a need for a more general and gradual introduction to language: transitional texts which will ease people into an understanding of complex ideas. This series of introductions is designed to serve this need.

Their purpose, therefore, is not to supplant but to support the more academically oriented introductions to linguistics: to prepare the conceptual ground. They are based on the belief that it is an advantage to have a broad map of the terrain sketched out before one considers its more specific features on a smaller scale, a general context in reference to which the detail makes sense. It is sometimes the case that students are introduced to detail without it being made clear what it is a detail *of*. Clearly, a general understanding of ideas is not sufficient: there needs to be closer scrutiny. But equally, close scrutiny can be myopic and meaningless unless it is related to the larger view. Indeed it can be said that the precondition of more particular enquiry is an awareness of what, in general, the particulars are about. This series is designed to provide this large-scale view of different areas of language study. As such it can serve as preliminary to (and precondition for) the more specific and specialized enquiry which students of linguistics are required to undertake.

But the series is not only intended to be helpful to such students. There are many people who take an interest in language without being academically engaged in linguistics *per se*. Such people may recognize the importance of understanding language for their own lines of enquiry, or for their own practical purposes, or quite simply for making them aware of something which figures so centrally in their everyday lives. If linguistics has revealing and relevant things to say about language, this should presumably not be a privileged revelation, but one accessible to people other than linguists. These books have been so designed as to accommodate these broader interests too: they are meant to be introductions to language more generally as well as to linguistics as a discipline.

Design

The books in the series are all cut to the same basic pattern. There are four parts: Survey, Readings, References, and Glossary.

Survey

This is a summary overview of the main features of the area of language study concerned: its scope and principles of enquiry, its basic concerns and key concepts. These are expressed and explained in ways which are intended to make them as accessible as possible to people who have no prior knowledge or expertise in the subject. The Survey is written to be readable and is uncluttered by the customary scholarly references. In this sense, it is simple. But it is not simplistic. Lack of specialist expertise does not imply an inability to understand or evaluate ideas. Ignorance means lack of knowledge, not lack of intelligence. The Survey, therefore, is meant to be challenging. It draws a map of the subject area in such a way as to stimulate thought and to invite a critical participation in the exploration of ideas. This kind of conceptual cartography has its dangers of course: the selection of what is significant, and the manner of its representation, will not be to the liking of everybody, particularly not, perhaps, to some of those inside the discipline. But these surveys are written in the belief that there must be an alternative to a technical account on the one hand, and an idiot's guide on the other if linguistics is to be made relevant to people in the wider world.

Readings

Some people will be content to read, and perhaps re-read, the summary Survey. Others will want to pursue the subject and so will use the Survey as the preliminary for more detailed study. The Readings provide the necessary transition. For here the reader is presented with texts extracted from the specialist literature. The purpose of these Readings is quite different from the Survey. It is to get readers to focus on the specifics of what is said, and how it is said, in these source texts. Questions are provided to further this purpose: they are designed to direct attention to points in each text, how they compare across texts, and how they deal with the issues discussed in the Survey. The idea is to give readers an initial familiarity with the more specialist idiom of the linguistics literature, where the issues might not be so readily accessible, and to encourage them into close critical reading.

References

One way of moving into more detailed study is through the Readings. Another is through the annotated References in the third section of each book. Here there is a selection of works (books and articles) for further reading. Accompanying comments indicate how these deal in more detail with the issues discussed in the different chapters of the Survey.

Glossary

Certain terms in the Survey appear in bold. These are terms used in a special or technical sense in the discipline. Their meanings are made clear in the discussion, but they are also explained in the Glossary at the end of each book. The Glossary is cross-referenced to the Survey, and therefore serves at the same time as an index. This enables readers to locate the term and what it signifies in the more general discussion, thereby, in effect, using the Survey as a summary work of reference.

Use

The series has been designed so as to be flexible in use. Each title is separate and self-contained, with only the basic format in common. The four sections of the format, as described here, can be drawn upon and combined in different ways, as required by the needs, or interests, of different readers. Some may be content with the Survey and the Glossary and may not want to follow up the suggested References. Some may not wish to venture into the Readings. Again, the Survey might be considered as appropriate preliminary reading for a course in applied linguistics or teacher education, and the Readings more appropriate for seminar discussion during the course. In short, the notion of an introduction will mean different things to different people, but in all cases the concern is to provide access to specialist knowledge and stimulate an awareness of its significance. This series as a whole has been designed to provide this access and promote this awareness in respect to different areas of language study.

H. G. WIDDOWSON

Author's acknowledgements

The fact that the *Oxford Introductions to Language Study* include a volume on historical linguistics bears witness to the fact that this time-honoured linguistic discipline has taken up a central place within the field again. This book tries to make the subject accessible to the uninitiated reader and to show how closely historical linguistics is linked to the other linguistic areas covered in the series. My thanks go to Oxford University Press and the series editor, H.G. Widdowson, for including this volume in the series.

Quite a number of people have provided me with valuable input and have helped to make this a better and more readable book.

First and foremost, I owe a very special debt of gratitude to H.G. Widdowson for his continuous support and invaluable advice through all the stages of my writing; he has made numerous proposals for improvement, both in regard to the overall structure of the book and to countless details, and has painstakingly read through the various drafts of the manuscript.

The following friends and colleagues have read the whole or substantial parts of the manuscript in various stages and have made valuable suggestions: Clausdirk Pollner, Hans Platzer, Angelika Hirsch, Ute Smit, Barbara Seidlhofer, Gunther Kaltenböck. Nikolaus Ritt provided me with valuable information on neo–Darwinian evolutionary theory. My heartfelt thanks to all of them. I am much indebted to the people at Oxford University Press for all their support. Last, but not least, my special thanks go to my wife, who has not only read both the manuscript and the proofs, but has also been a constant source of encouragement.

HERBERT SCHENDL
London, October 2000

Survey

1
Language change as a matter of fact

All physical aspects of the universe and all aspects of human life are subject to change, and languages are no exception. Individual changes can be quite abrupt and obvious, as when new words make an appearance and become popular. Normally, however, language change is gradual, almost imperceptible, as with the slow alterations in pronunciation when one generation speaks slightly differently from another. Linguistic changes tend to be the result of two equivalent forms coexisting as variants for some time, and one giving way to the other. Two words, for example, or two ways of pronouncing the same word, may coexist in the same speech community for some time, but may be used by different sub-groups or on different occasions. However, for reasons to be discussed later, such variant forms may begin to compete, and finally one will dominate and the other decline.

Small linguistic changes may be evident in everyday experience, and people may notice (and sometimes disapprove) when words are used or pronounced in different ways; but language change is most obvious on a large scale when we look at older texts of a particular language, and the further back we go in history, the more obvious the changes become. Here is an example of Old English, taken from the time of King Alfred the Great (late ninth century AD), for which a translation in modern English is given below:

(1) Ælfred kyning hateð gretan Wærferð biscep his wordum luflice ond freondlice ond ðe cyðan hate, ðæt me com swiðe oft on gemynd, hwelce wiotan iu wæron giond Angelcynn ægðer ge godcundra hada ge woruldcundra, ond hu gesæliglica tida ða wæron giond Angelcynn.

[King Alfred sends greetings to Bishop Wærferth with his loving and friendly words, and I would declare to you that it has very often come to my mind what wise men there were formerly throughout the English people, both in sacred and in secular orders, and how there were happy times then throughout England.]

Here the language has changed almost out of all recognition. A linguistic discussion of the passage would go beyond the scope of this introduction, but it is evident that only a small number of words of the modern language still carry obvious traces of their heredity, and even these have changed in various ways, e.g. *freondlice, luflice > friendly, lovely.* Some of the letters used have disappeared from modern English, such as ð for modern *th*, or æ for the vowel in modern standard English *hat*.

And here is an example from Middle English, almost half of a millennium later, taken from the Prologue of Chaucer's *Canterbury Tales*:

(2) Ye goon to Caunterbury—God yow speede,
The blisful martir quite yow youre meede!
And wel I woot, as ye goon by the weye,
Ye shapen yow to talen and to pleye;
For trewely, confort ne myrthe is noon
To ride by the weye doumb as a stoon;

The language here is less remote. There are obviously several differences in spelling, for example, the endings of verbs (*goon, talen,* both with plural ending -(*e*)*n*), and in some word forms (*woot* 'know', *ye* 'you'). If you heard the passage read aloud, the distance from modern English would be somewhat greater. But most of the features in (2) we can recognize as related to the English language as we use it today.

And, finally, here is a passage from Shakespeare's *A Midsummer Night's Dream* (III. ii. 335) written about two centuries after Chaucer, at the end of the sixteenth century.

(3) *Lysander* Now she holds me not.
Now follow, if thou dar'st, to try whose right,
Of thine or mine, is most in Helena.
Demetrius Follow! Nay, I'll go with thee, cheek by jowl.

Hermia You, mistress, all this coil is long of you: Nay, go not
back.
Helena I will not trust you, I,
No longer stay in your curst company.
Your hands than mine are quicker for a fray;
My legs are longer, though, to run away.

This is in many ways, including the pronunciation, very close
to modern English. But there are still obvious differences on all
linguistic levels, especially with regard to grammar and vocabulary. In the second person singular of verbs, we notice the ending
-*st* in *dar'st* and the singular personal pronouns *thou/thee* besides
you. The negative sentence *she holds me not* would be expressed
in modern English as *she does not hold me*, and the word order of
Your hands than mine are quicker for a fray sounds definitely
peculiar today. None of the words looks particularly unusual,
although in some cases their meanings have changed. The word
coil, for example, will be familiar to many because it also occurs
in Hamlet's famous phrase 'shuffled off this mortal coil'. But they
will almost certainly not know its sixteenth-century meaning of
'turmoil'.

In looking at a particular language over a longer period of
time, it becomes apparent that language change does not result in
different distinct stages of a language but in a historical continuum, so that speakers easily understand the language of the
generations immediately before and after them, but meet
increasing difficulties in understanding chronologically remote
stages of their language. This closely resembles the well-known
phenomenon of the dialect continuum: adjacent geographical
varieties of a language are mutually intelligible, but dialect
speakers may have problems with geographically remote varieties
of their language. The close relationship between temporal and
spatial linguistic differences may also be noticeable in another
respect: thus, travelling through rural Britain from south to north
or from east to west can in many ways resemble a journey
through the history of English, since rural dialects have often
preserved older forms of language.

Linguistic change, then, is not restricted to particular languages or generations, but is a universal fact. This does not mean
that people will always be happy to accept the inevitable.

Attitudes to language change

Language is so closely associated with social identity that it is not surprising that people have strong feelings about it. Language change can be unsettling and a widespread attitude is to see it as a change for the worse. Speakers of different periods and cultures have often tended to think that their own language is inferior to that of their forebears. For them, language change is a matter of decline or decay. In some societies this attitude can be traced back to the biblical account of the Tower of Babel. Here the change from one common language to a diversity of different languages is presented as divine punishment for sinful behaviour.

In the history of European languages, negative statements on language change as corruption and decay clearly predominate over neutral ones, while positive views seem to be conspicuously absent. In most of the emerging European national languages we find increasing attempts to 'purify' and codify the language, i.e. to fix prescriptive rules of correct usage and thus to stop language change. This task was partly undertaken by official institutions, so-called 'language academies', such as the Accademia della Crusca in Florence (founded in 1582), the French Académie française (1635), and various German 'language societies' of the seventeenth and eighteenth centuries. In England the eighteenth century, with its striving for regularity and order, was especially hostile to the idea of linguistic change, but here **codification** was mainly carried out by influential individuals. Many of the leading intellectual and literary figures of the period, such as Jonathan Swift and Samuel Johnson, vehemently opposed the idea of language change. For Johnson, author of the famous *Dictionary of the English Language* (1755), for instance, all linguistic change was 'of itself an evil'. In the Preface to his *Dictionary*, he states:

(4) tongues [i.e. languages], like governments, have a natural tendency to degeneration; we have long preserved our constitution, let us make some struggles for our language.

This comparison of language with human institutions like governments was in no way restricted to England. For the American politician Benjamin Franklin, language reflected social reality and the supposed 'degeneration' of language directly mirrored the degeneration of contemporary society.

This 'complaint tradition' (as it has been called) has continued up to the present century. Here is a recent example from a popular book on linguistic correctness by an American art critic, expressing a view echoed by educated laypersons in many countries. (See also Section 2, Readings, Text 1.)

(5) [B]y and large, linguistic changes are caused by the ignorance of speakers and writers, and in the last few centuries—given our schools, dictionaries, and books on grammar—such ignorance could have been, like the live nettle or poison ivy it is, uprooted.
(John Simon, *Paradigms Lost*, 1976)

Not only individuals, but also governmental institutions have shown emotional or ideologically motivated attitudes towards certain changes. In Nazi Germany attempts were made to assert the integrity of the language by promoting words of German character even for established foreign words (*Fernsprecher* 'telephone', literally 'distant speaker', instead of *Telephon*). But even democratic governments are not immune from nationalistic tendencies in trying to stop excessive borrowing of foreign words. A recent case in point has been the French government's (unsuccessful) measures against the use of 'franglais', English borrowings such as *le weekend* and *le shopping*, by means of governmental decrees and attempts to replace them with French words coined by an official committee, e.g. *le baladeur* for *le walkman*. Though reversion to a real or imagined earlier (and 'purer') state of language also involves change, this type of change is seen to be 'in the right direction' and acceptable for political reasons.

Even professional linguists have in the past been prone to a conservative attitude to language change. Early nineteenth-century scholars regarded language as a growing organism with a stage of growth, a brief moment of evolutionary perfection, and subsequent decay. Thus, for example, the disappearance of case inflections between Old English and Modern English or from Latin to French, and their partial replacement by prepositional phrases (for example, Old English *freondes* vs. English *of the friend*; Latin *amici* vs. French *de l'ami* 'of the friend') was seen as indicating a decline.

Contemporary linguists in general hold a neutral or even positive attitude towards change. On the positive side it has been claimed that changes are a necessary development to make languages more communicatively effective as they become attuned to changing social needs. This also applies to the promotion of conscious linguistic changes to achieve this goal, such as language planning and measures to make language 'politically correct' (cf. Chapter 8). Furthermore, changes have been viewed as necessary therapeutic measures to restore the balance and symmetry of the linguistic system, or as moves towards the simplification of the grammar. In such a view, the change of language over periods of time is a function of influences operating at any given time. In this respect, the study of history (of language or of anything else) depends on an understanding of the present, just as the present is to be understood by reference to the past.

Language state and process

Nevertheless, in much modern linguistics past and present have been separated into different areas of enquiry. It has been a common assumption that **synchronic** linguistics, which concerns itself with the state of languages at a given time, in particular the present, is most conveniently carried out in disregard of the findings of historical or **diachronic** linguistics about the processes of language development over time. However, this strict division is based on a misunderstanding of the relationship between these two aspects of the study of language. On the one hand, the synchronic study of linguistic systems can provide insights that can be used in reconstructing their past. On the other hand, we should also recognize that the implied assumption that synchronic linguistic systems are completely systematic, static, and homogeneous, is a fiction. All of them are in some respect *un*systematic: the numerous irregular relics of earlier systems (the 'exceptions' to the rule), which are simply inexplicable in synchronic terms, can only be explained by reference to past states and developments. The unstable state of a language at any given point of time is the consequence of historical processes, and its very instability is evidence that these processes continue to operate in the present.

Equally, there is a close interrelationship between synchronic linguistic variation, i.e. the coexistence of more or less equivalent variants at a given time, and diachronic linguistic change. The growing awareness of these facts over the past thirty years has led to a major reorientation in the discipline, with historical linguistics again taking its rightful place in the field of language study.

The aims and scope of historical linguistics

The beginning of historical linguistic studies in the modern sense of the word dates back more than two hundred years, though there is a much older tradition of language study in some cultures. So it is not surprising that there have been very different scholarly traditions and approaches to historical linguistics, each of which sets particular research objectives and calls for different methodologies. We can identify these broad areas of enquiry:

1 The study of the *history* of particular languages on the basis of existing written data.
2 The study of the *prehistory* of languages by means of **comparative reconstruction**, whereby the unrecorded past is inferred on the evidence of the data that *are* available from a later period.
3 The study of *ongoing changes* in a language, i.e. changes happening at the present time.

However fascinating these issues may be in their own right (especially for historical linguists themselves) they should be linked to other and more abstract aims, namely the discovery of more general, possibly universal, aspects of language change. By relating the descriptive facts about a particular language to what is common across all (or most) other languages, the historical linguist seeks to explain *why* languages change, and *how* these changes spread in space and time. The most promising area for finding answers to these questions is the study of ongoing changes, especially when carried out within a framework which emphasizes the interrelationship between social factors, synchronic linguistic variation at any one time, and diachronic linguistic change over time.

2

Reconstructing the past: data and evidence

The data of historical linguistics

The synchronic description of living languages in the present can be based on a wide range of data, such as the introspection of the linguist (as a native speaker), the guided elicitation of data from native informants, and observation (including the use of corpora). Different linguistic schools have placed different emphases on these types of data. The data of historical linguistics, on the other hand, are much more restricted. Obviously, much of the past is not accessible through introspection or elicitation. We only have its observable traces to go on, most importantly the limited corpus of written texts as a record of actual language use in former times.

Fortunately, many languages have a long recorded past, which provides evidence for the development of the individual languages and also for more general properties of linguistic change. But there are clear limitations with regard to both the quantity and the quality of the data. In general, the further back we go in time, the more sparse and unreliable the data become, while at the same time the language becomes more and more remote. Frequently we lack sufficient extralinguistic information on old texts, such as their author, purpose, or audience. Equally, the range of text types is limited, and authentic spoken data are altogether lacking before the twentieth century. The reconstruction of older written language is difficult enough, but it is even more difficult to reconstruct older speech from written data.

We must bear in mind too that this reconstruction is not a straightforward matter of facts. The interpretation—and even the selection—of the available data is always informed by underlying general assumptions about language or a specific theory to which the historical linguist subscribes. This means that, as with other aspects of history, we will find competing explanations of the past.

Whenever the beginning of human language may have been— and most modern estimates vary between 50,000 and 100,000 years ago, though some extend it substantially to one million years ago or even more—it is obvious that the evolution of language is documented only for a very small percentage of its total history, and even this applies only to relatively few of the 5,000 to 6,000 human languages said to exist in the world at present. The lack of data from these unrecorded stages, i.e. from the prehistory of languages, can however be partly overcome by a systematic comparison of the oldest written records of related languages even if they are now extinct. These can be as fascinating as dinosaur eggs or fossils of extinct species and, just like these witnesses of the past, they can help us to extend our knowledge of linguistic evolution further back into prehistoric and unrecorded time. The reconstruction of the prehistory of languages is the domain of comparative reconstruction discussed later in this chapter.

The written evidence

Written texts provide the most important data for historical linguistics, and it is a crucial matter how these data are interpreted as evidence for earlier spoken language as well as for linguistic systems. Such interpretation may present almost insurmountable difficulties in the case of extinct languages with unknown writing systems. The deciphering of extinct languages written in such systems often depends on the existence of bi- or trilingual texts, in which at least one of the languages is known. A famous case in point is the Rosetta Stone found in the course of Napoleon's expedition to Egypt and now in the British Museum: the trilingual inscription on this stone in ancient Greek alongside two different versions of the ancient Egyptian script provided the key to the decipherment of the Egyptian hieroglyphs.

But interpreting written data as evidence of language systems and speech is not unproblematic, even for languages whose writing systems are known and well established. Consider alphabetic writing as used for English and the other European languages. Whereas in other writing systems symbols might stand for syllables or words, here they represent sounds, i.e. vowels and consonants, more or less directly, whether in the Latin, Greek, or Cyrillic alphabet. These alphabets stand in a long tradition and their basic writing conventions have been handed down for centuries. But even so, the nature of the correspondences between 'letters' and 'sounds' is by no means easy to determine. Speech and writing are two distinct though clearly related systems, but the nature of this relationship may change over time. It is widely agreed that alphabetic writing initially aimed at rendering the distinctive sound units of a language and tended to neglect non-distinctive differences: thus the letter *r* in Latin, Old English, Old French, etc. represents the distinctive unit /r/ (as opposed to /l/, /m/, etc.), but does not tell us anything about its specific realization as a trilled, retroflex, or guttural sound (cf. the different quality of /r/ in English, Scots, French or German).

Furthermore, it is safe to assume that the scribes who first used the Latin alphabet to write down languages such as Old English or Old High German adhered to the Latin spelling conventions, since they had been first trained in writing Latin. Fortunately, these conventions are quite well known as a result of the unbroken Latin tradition in Western civilization. However, the Latin writing system had to be adapted in a number of ways to these newly written languages. For example, Latin did not have a sound corresponding to the initial sound in English *thing*, while Old English did. Here, the Old English scribes adopted two alternative solutions: they either used a letter from the old runic alphabet, namely þ , or they slightly changed the Latin letter *d* into the form ð.

The originally more-or-less direct relationship between letters and sounds, or more generally, between writing and speech became, however, blurred as a result of language change, since spelling tends to be conservative and either does not record changes at all or does so only after a considerable time-lag. An additional complicating factor may be the mixing of different regional or national spelling conventions due to cultural contact. Thus Anglo-Norman conventions appear widespread in English texts after the Norman invasion of England in 1066. To give a simple example from the history of English: the Old and Middle English forms of *house* were both pronounced with long /uː/ (the vowel in modern English *goose*) and the Old English spelling *hus* for /huːs/ reflects the original Latin-based one-to-one relation between speech and writing. The new Middle English spelling *hous(e)* for the same pronunciation /huːs/ is due to the adoption of the Anglo-Norman convention of writing *ou* for /uː/ (cf. modern French *jour* 'day', *pour* 'for'). This spelling is still retained today, though /uː/ was diphthongized in the Early Modern period, yielding modern English /haʊs/. We can say that English writing started as a system which was secondary to, i.e. dependent on, speech, but became increasingly autonomous and unrelated to actual pronunciation. (For the relation between writing and speech see also Readings, Text 3.)

Sources of evidence

The hypotheses of the historical linguist depend crucially on the interpretation of the data. It is not just a matter of the amount of data available but primarily of their quality. To evaluate the quality of old texts, we have to find out as much as possible about their extralinguistic context (such as the author, scribe, purpose, and location of a text, etc.), and about the textual tradition, including the original form and date of composition and copying. This is the task of the philologist, for whom auxiliary disciplines such as history and palaeography, the study of ancient writing, are of major importance.

Only very few old texts are in the author's own hand, and even these may show various kinds of textual errors. Mostly they are the result of multiple copying by different scribes in different regions and over a long period of time. Some texts are compilations by a specific author from linguistically divergent, possibly orally transmitted original sources, as with Homer's *Iliad* and *Odyssey*, or the *Rigveda*, the oldest collection of religious texts written in Sanskrit. Such textual history may result in linguistically composite texts with a mixed language, full of scribal errors due to negligence or insufficient competence in the language(s) or varieties of the original. These different linguistic layers, whether dialectal or diachronic, must be disentangled and scribal errors detected before the text can be used as data for forming hypotheses about specific stages of a language. Furthermore, old texts are often translations, e.g. from Latin into Old English, or from Greek into early Gothic or Old Church Slavic, so that we have to reckon with linguistic influence from the original language.

Though written texts constitute the major source for historical linguistics, other types of data may provide important supplementary evidence. For example, archaeological findings such as pieces of pottery, grave findings, and other historical material have contributed substantially to our knowledge of the settlement history of early Anglo-Saxon England, which again may help in reconstructing the dialectal distribution of Old English.

Of particular interest as data are direct descriptions of and explicit comments on a language by contemporary speakers. Such 'metalinguistic' evidence is, however, rare for the early stages of most languages and not always reliable, though there are excellent early grammars of Sanskrit, Greek, and Latin. The bulk of such information for European languages only dates from the modern period. Some detailed descriptions of English sounds and even phonetic transcriptions of texts date back to the sixteenth century and we have numerous surviving glossaries, word lists, and translations of Latin and other languages, which provide information about word meanings in medieval Europe.

Last but not least, modern dialects and related languages can provide valuable information to help construct or test our hypotheses.

Let us now look at how data are used to reconstruct linguistic history.

Comparing and reconstructing languages

A basic hypothesis in historical linguistics is that for all their current differences languages may originate from one common source (or **proto-language**), to which they are thus **genetically related**. We have unambiguous linguistic and extralinguistic historical evidence for such genetic relationships in the case of the modern Romance languages (French, Italian, Spanish, Catalan, Portuguese, Romanian, etc.). These are the direct descendants or daughter languages of Latin (more precisely of its different spoken forms, Vulgar Latin), from which they have evolved in the course of centuries as a result of geographical distance and isolation, social factors and political developments, and through contact with other languages. Genetically related languages form **language families** and they show systematic and recurrent formal correspondences, i.e. similarities and differences which are too regular and frequent to be mere chance or the result of borrowing. These correspondences become more evident and regular the further back we go in language history. They are, for example, stronger between Old French and Old Spanish than between Modern French and Modern Spanish.

The most famous and best-researched language family is the Indo-European (IE) one, with a long textual tradition in a wide range of geographically divergent daughter languages. Indo-European languages have long been spoken from India to the western borders of the European continent, and have in more recent times been exported all over the world. They are grouped into a number of subfamilies (or branches) such as Germanic, Italic (including Latin and the Romance languages), Balto-Slavic (including the Slavic languages Russian, Czech, Bulgarian, etc.), Celtic, Greek, and Indo-Iranian (with Persian, Kurdish, Sanskrit and a number of modern Indian languages). The reconstruction of the common ancestor of these languages, Proto-Indo-European, was one of the outstanding achievements of nineteenth-century comparative linguistics.

The most widely used way of showing genetic relationships graphically is the **family tree** model. The diagram on the next page gives a simplified family tree of the Germanic languages, which disregards intermediate stages such as Old Norse as the common ancestor of Icelandic and Norwegian, and the older stages of the modern languages such as Old English, Old High German, etc.

Linguists vary in their interpretation of the informational value of such family trees. For some this is only a convenient way of visualizing the degree of genetic relationship between languages, and labels such as North Germanic are seen as a cover term for a group of languages showing closer similarities between

Family tree of Germanic languages

each other than with the other languages of the family. For others (and this was how it was first conceived) this is a model of linguistic change which directly shows the way in which proto-languages diversify into daughter languages. In such a view a label such as North Germanic stands for an actual language, an ancestor which acted as an intermediate proto-language. (For an alternative to the family tree model, see Readings, Text 4.)

Correspondences between languages

The comparative reconstruction that enables us to establish such language families is based on identifying correspondences between related languages. These correspondences are most evident on the levels of phonology and morphology, i.e. sounds and inflections, and are accessible through the systematic comparison of so-called **cognates**. These are words which are similar both in form and meaning and which go back to a common source. Cognates are particularly frequent in the basic vocabulary of daughter languages, since words which relate to basic aspects of life or to common human experience (such as time, place, food, or social relations) tend to be less readily replaced by borrowings from other languages.

The following simple example demonstrates the basic principles of comparative reconstruction. French *champ*, Italian *campo*, Spanish and Portuguese *campo* all derive from Latin *campus* 'field' and are thus cognates. Even if Latin had not been preserved in a wealth of written records, we could partly reconstruct it by comparing such cognate forms of its daughter languages, as illustrated in the table below (the meanings of the respective words in English are (1) 'dear' (2) 'field' (3) 'house').

Correspondences between Latin and Romance languages

	Latin	French	Italian	Spanish	Portuguese
1	*carus* [k]	*cher* [ʃɛr]	*caro* [k]	*caro* [k]	*caro* [k]
2	*campus* [k]	*champ* [ʃɑ̃]	*campo* [k]	*campo* [k]	*campo* [k]
3	*casa* [k]	*chez* [ʃe] 'at'	*casa* [k]	*casa* [k]	*casa* [k]

The table above shows three sets of cognates from four different Romance languages, as well as the Latin form. Having established the sets on the basis of their similarities of form and meaning, we now proceed to reconstruct the original sounds of the proto-form of each set. For this purpose we establish systematic sound correspondences within and between the sets of cognates: in all three sets, for example, the French initial consonant [ʃ] (as in English *shoe*) corresponds to [k] in the three other Romance languages. There are evidently three possible sources for these initial consonants in the common proto-language: (i) it was [k] as preserved in Italian, Spanish, and Portuguese; in this case, the original sound would have undergone a change only in French; or (ii) it was original [ʃ] as in French, in which case it would have changed into [k] in the other three languages; or (iii) it was neither [k] nor [ʃ], but another consonant from which the two attested ones developed as a result of different sound changes. As is evident from these hypotheses, the reconstruction of the proto-sound also involves reconstructing the sound changes which occurred in the individual daughter languages.

There are certain general methodological principles that we can bring to bear on deciding on the proto-sound. The most important of these are:

(i) Any reconstruction should involve sound changes that are phonetically plausible. The phonetic plausibility of a change is evaluated on the basis of general phonetic considerations as to how sounds are formed as well as on the extensive documentation of sound changes in other languages. On this evidence, a change from [k] to [ʃ] is more frequent and plausible (and thus more 'natural') than a change in the opposite direction, [ʃ] > [k]. It is even more natural if it proceeds via an intermediate stage [tʃ], whose existence is well documented in the history of French. This stage is also reflected in early English borrowings from older French such as *Charles*, *chief*, which have preserved this earlier French pronunciation with [tʃ]. On the basis of this principle of phonetic plausibility or 'naturalness' we reconstruct *[k] as the initial consonant of the above sets 1–3 for Proto-Romance, in which the asterisk * indicates a reconstructed form, without written evidence.

(ii) A second, though less reliable principle, is the 'majority principle'. Any reconstruction should involve as few changes between the proto-language and its daughter languages as possible. Thus, the sound which is more frequently met in the related forms is more likely to be the original one. In sets 1–3, three languages have [k], while only one has [ʃ]. The reconstructed proto-sound *[k] is not only more frequently found in the corresponding sets, but also involves only one sound change in the history of the daughter languages (for French), while in the case of reconstructed *[ʃ] three languages would have undergone the same change *[ʃ] > [k].

Continuing with our reconstruction in this manner will eventually result for sets 1–3 in the Proto-Romance forms *caro*, *campo*, *casa*, although this reconstruction is not always as easy and straightforward as with *[k]. These reconstructed Proto-Romance forms are quite close to the attested Latin forms given in the table (as an inflected language, Latin actually had the case forms *caro*, *campo*).

In the case of the Romance languages we are obviously in the fortunate position of being able to verify our reconstructions to a large extent, and thus to test our methodology and basic assumptions. In general, however, we can only reconstruct those features of the proto-language which have left at least some trace in one of the daughter languages. Thus the quality of our reconstruction crucially depends on the quality of the surviving evidence.

At the same time, the individual reconstructed sounds must also form a plausible complete system, which should furthermore conform to more general principles of sound systems. Languages tend to have symmetrically structured sound systems and there would have to be compelling evidence to disregard this general tendency for a reconstructed proto-language. To illustrate this with an example or two: a language having a set of so-called 'voiceless stops', i.e. [p, t, k], and the corresponding 'voiced stops' [b, d, g] is more likely (or natural) than one with [p, t, k] but only [b, g], i.e. without [d]—though gaps in a system do occur in natural languages. Similarly, there are no known languages which have only nasal vowels (as in French *champ*, cf. above) and no 'pure', i.e. non-nasal vowels, and only very few which have no nasal consonants. Such general 'typological' considerations must influence the final shape of any reconstruction.

We should note here that there are certain reservations about this method of analysis. In the first place, the reconstructed proto-language is (mis)represented as an idealized homogeneous system, whereas in fact natural languages are necessarily heterogeneous and variable. Secondly, sound changes are presented as being regular and occurring without exception in all identical contexts. As we shall see later, both these views have come under attack in recent decades, though the main results of comparative reconstruction, i.e. most of its hypotheses about the shape of a number of proto-languages, have stood the test of time. (For a discussion of the status of reconstructed forms, see Readings, Text 2.)

Laws of change

In the reconstruction of linguistic relationships and developments we identify certain processes of change that are so regular as to be considered laws. One of these is evident in the development of the Germanic branch of Indo-European.

The Germanic languages show a series of distinctive and related sound changes involving certain Indo-European consonants. These are accounted for by Grimm's Law, named after the German linguist who discovered it. It states that Indo-European stops, i.e. consonants produced with a brief closure such as [p, b, t, d, k, g], regularly changed into different consonants (the stops [p, t, k], for example, becoming the fricatives [f, θ, x], i.e consonants produced with an audible friction due to the narrowing of two speech organs; see Chapter 5 for phonetic details). More specifically, Grimm's Law states the following ('>' stands for 'develop into'; 'voiced/voiceless' refers to the presence or absence of vibration of the vocal folds; 'aspirated' refers to an audible breath):

> voiceless stops [p, t, k] > voiceless fricatives [f, θ, x]
> voiced stops [b, d, g] > voiceless stops [p, t, k]
> voiced aspirated stops [bh, dh, gh] > voiced plain stops [b, d, g]

This law applies to all Germanic languages. Other Indo-European languages, such as Greek or Sanskrit, basically show the original sounds of Proto-Indo-European. This may be seen in the following table, which gives (i) one example each of two changes of voiceless stops to voiceless fricatives ([p > f], [t > θ]) and of voiced stops to voiceless stops ([d > t], [g > k]) in three old Germanic languages (Gothic, Old English 'OE', Old High German 'OHG'), (ii) examples of their preservation in two non-Germanic Indo-European languages (Sanskrit and Latin), and (iii) the reconstructed Proto-Indo-European ('PrIE') forms.

Reflexes of the working of Grimm's Law

Sanskrit	Latin	Gothic	OE	OHG	PrIE	
pād-	*ped-*	*fotus*	*fōt*	*fuoz*	**p*	'foot'
tráyas	*trēs*	*þrija* /θ/	*þrīe* /θ/	*drī*	**t*	'three'
dvā(u)-	*duo*	*twai*	*twā*	*zwā* /ts/	**d*	'two'
jánas	*genus*	*kuni*	*cyn* /k/	*kunni*	**g*	'race, kin'

As shown above, comparative reconstruction is based on consideration of related forms in genetically related languages. Its basic methodology can, however, also be used to reconstruct unattested earlier stages or gaps in the tradition of a language by comparing related forms from *within* a single language. This is the domain of **internal reconstruction**, which relies on the linguistic traces left in a language from its earlier stages.

Internal reconstruction

All languages show patterned alternations in different realizations of **morphemes**, the smallest meaningful units of language. Thus the English regular plural morpheme is realized in three different variants (or allomorphs), namely /-s/, /-z/ and /ɪz/, cf. *cats* [kæts], *dogs* [dɒgz], *horses* [hɔːsɪz]. Internal reconstruction starts from the assumption that such synchronic alternation is in general the result of regular sound changes and that the different forms have developed from a single non-alternating form. A simple example to illustrate this is German words ending in voiceless stops. While some of these, such as *Rat* [t] 'advice' and *Lack* [k] 'varnish', retain the voiceless stop in inflected forms, others such as *Rad* [t] 'bicycle' and *Tag* [k] 'day' show alternation between a voiceless stop in word-final position and a voiced one in the inflected forms (as in *Rades, Tages*, with the genitive singular ending in *-es*).

[raːt]	[raːtəs]	'advice'	[raːt]	[raːdəs]	'bicycle'
[lak]	[lakəs]	'varnish'	[taːk]	[taːgəs]	'day'

The non-alternating ancestor of the variants [raːt/raːd-] and [taːk/taːg-] of the morphemes meaning 'bicycle' and 'day' could have been either (i) [raːt], [taːk], (ii) [raːd], [taːg], or (iii) an unattested different form. Since internal reconstruction should follow the same basic principles applied in comparative reconstruction, the hypothetical changes leading to the alternations should fulfil the criteria of economy and naturalness, and should not lead to contradictory results in other forms. Looking at the sound system of German, we notice that voiced stops never occur in word-final position, so that it is plausible to reconstruct the earlier non-alternating single forms with the voiced stops *[taːg] 'day' and *[raːd] 'bicycle' and a subsequent sound change of **devoicing** voiced stops in word-final position, while the voiced stops remain in non-final positions. We have thus reconstructed both the original non-alternating forms *[taːg/taːgəs] and the sound change of final devoicing, which has led to the modern alternations [taːk/taːgəs]. Of course, internal reconstruction is not always as straightforward as this. There are alternations which are much more complex and where the original state has been obscured by multiple sound changes. In such cases, the reconstruction also has to establish the

relative chronology of the various changes, i.e. the order in which they have taken place. However, if a specific change has left no trace in the language, internal reconstruction may lead to a grossly simplified description of the intermediate stages. Furthermore, we need to note that not all alternations can be traced back to a single non-alternating form.

Internal reconstruction is most fruitfully applied in cases where we have insufficient material for comparative reconstruction, as in the case of **isolates**, i.e. languages with no known relatives, or when only very distant, possibly controversial relatives exist. In such cases as well as with languages without any textual tradition, internal reconstruction may be virtually the only way to learn about the unattested linguistic past. Otherwise, it should ideally be used in combination with other methods such as comparative reconstruction.

The present chapter has shown how the historical linguist—much like an archaeologist—can piece together information even on unrecorded stages of languages and processes of change. These methods have been most successfully applied to phonology and morphology, while syntactic reconstruction is more controversial. The reconstruction of the proto-vocabulary in core areas such as kinship, plants, animals and metals has also increased our knowledge of the societal structures, the economic organization, and the original homeland of the Indo-Europeans.

Let us now turn to a more detailed consideration of linguistic change at the different levels of language.

3
Vocabulary change

For the convenience of analysis, linguists divide linguistic systems into different levels: sounds (phonology), word structure (morphology), sentence structure (syntax) and meaning (semantics). Linguistic change occurs at all levels, and changes on one level may influence another level and trigger off changes there as well. Thus sound change can lead to loss of inflections, i.e. to morphological change, and this in turn may have consequences for syntactic structure, such as the flexibility of word order. This should be borne in mind in the following discussion of change at different levels of language. We will begin with the changes which are most obvious, namely those affecting vocabulary, and then proceed to the levels of morphology and syntax, where changes are in general slower and thus less obvious.

Speakers constantly have to adapt language to changing communicative needs in a changing environment. Thus new words are coined, old ones get their meanings extended, while on the other hand existing words or meanings constantly fall into disuse. The unparalleled and well-documented increase in the number of words and word meanings from Old English to the present day makes English particularly well suited for a discussion of lexical change.

There are two main strategies for the introduction of new words, namely **borrowing** from other languages and the coining of new words, i.e. the process of **word-formation**. Languages may differ in their preference for one or the other of these processes, though most if not all use both. Old English, for example, only had about three per cent of borrowed or **loan words**, while 70 per cent of modern English is said to consist of loan words from more than 80 different languages, primarily Latin and French.

There are obvious historical reasons for this extensive borrowing, such as the Norman Conquest of England in 1066 and the high prestige of Latin as the international language of communication up to the eighteenth century. But it is ultimately the attitude of speakers towards foreign influence in general and towards specific languages in particular which determines the acceptance and degree of borrowing. Since borrowing is the result of language contact, it will be discussed in more detail in Chapter 6. In the following sections, we will focus on the other strategies which speakers use to refer to new or changed concepts, namely the coining of new words and **semantic change**, i.e. change in word meaning.

Coining new words

As the smallest meaningful units of a language, morphemes constitute the basic building blocks of words. New words are normally formed by combining existing words and morphemes into new, complex words. English *teach* consists of a single morpheme, while *teach.er* can be analysed into two meaningful units. The suffix *-er*, which signifies 'agent' in *teacher*, and 'instrument' in *toaster*, is a so-called 'bound' morpheme, since it never occurs on its own.

When discussing historical word-formation, we must differentiate between the appearance of new words, i.e. the output of word-formation rules, and these abstract rules themselves. Word-formation rules are both language-specific and subject to diachronic change, especially in regard to their productivity, i.e. the frequency and flexibility with which they are used to coin new words.

Two of the most important word-formation processes are **compounding** and **affixation**. Compounds are the combination of two independent words, i.e. free morphemes, like *guesthouse* (< *guest* + *house*), while in affixation a bound morpheme is added to a base, as a prefix (e.g. *un.like*) or a suffix (*like.ness*).

Compounding has been highly productive throughout the history of English, and innumerable compounds were coined over the centuries. Many of these have survived since Old English times, such as *cynnes man* 'kinsman'; others have gone out of use, such as Old English *ceapman*, which was replaced by the French loan *merchant*, though it has survived in *chapman* as an archaism and as a surname. On the basis of the semantic relations between their different parts we can distinguish different subtypes of compounds, such as *guesthouse* 'house for guests' vs. *girlfriend* 'friend who is a girl'. Not all of these subtypes have been equally productive in the history of English and it is not too difficult to imagine compounds which are unacceptable in English. However, English, and German likewise, has definitely fewer constraints on compounding than some other languages such as French.

As a result of sound changes compounds may lose their transparency and develop into unanalysable simple words, such as Old English *godspell* 'good tidings' > *gospel*. Few non-specialists are aware that English *lord*, *lady* go back to the original compounds **hlaf-weard*, literally 'loaf-keeper', and *hlæfdiʒe*, literally 'loaf-kneader', etymologies which are also interesting sociologically as witnesses of the long tradition of keeping gender roles distinct.

Affixation has equally occurred throughout the history of English and before. A large number of prefixes and suffixes such as *un-*, *-ful*, *-ness* have remained productive since the Old English period, while some like *be-* and *-th* are now unproductive but have survived in established words such as *be.lieve*, *warm.th*, *leng.th*. Others have disappeared without trace, like Old English *-cund* 'of the nature of' (Old English *deofolcund* 'devilish'). Its meaning partly overlaps with that of modern English *-wise*, as in *crabwise*. After a long period of low productivity this suffix has become highly productive in recent times, especially in forming new adverbs such as *taxwise*, *talentwise*, *saleswise*, etc. Such forms were still considered 'bad English' by many British speakers only a few years ago, but they have now become widely accepted in informal speech—an obvious case of a recent change in productivity. On the other hand, Latin or French prefixes and suffixes such as *dis-*, *re-*, *en-/em-*; *-able*, *-age*, etc. were taken over in numerous loan words, especially from the thirteenth and fourteenth centuries onwards. In general, these affixes became productive in English only after some time, especially in new combinations with native English elements, as in *dislike* (1555), *eatable* (1483), *barnage* 'infancy' (1325), etc.

From Middle English onwards, the formation of phrasal verbs such as *get out, give up* steadily increased, possibly under Scandinavian and French influence. On the other hand, the Old English verbal compounds (with inseparable or with separable first element, the latter as still in German *aufgeben – Geben sie auf!* 'Give up') ceased to be productive and were gradually replaced by the new type, though both coexisted for some time, cf. *fare out* (1393) and *outfare* (1150), *go out* (1325) and *outgo* (Old English).

Among the patterns which either first emerged or substantially increased their productivity in the Middle and Early Modern English periods, **conversion** (or 'zero derivation') deserves special mention. This is the change of word class without the addition of a formal suffix, as from verb to noun (*to cheat > a cheat*), or from adjective or adverb to verb (*lower > to lower, up > to up*), a process which establishes a link between vocabulary and grammar.

Before the codification of the English lexicon in the eighteenth century, we frequently find synonymous new coinings employing both native and foreign patterns; thus verbs with the Romance suffix *-ize* appear alongside the native conversion type, e.g. *to equal* and *to equalize* (both first attested in 1590); *to civil* (1591) and *to civilize* (1601), etc. Similar competing formations are found in negation, such as *disthrone* (1591), *dethrone* (1609), and *unthrone* (1611) as synonymous negative forms of the verb *to enthrone*.

In modern English we increasingly find derivations from proper names, such as places of origin (*jersey*, from the Channel Island of that name; *coach*, from the Hungarian town *Kocs*, cf. also German *Kutsche*), or persons connected with new concepts or things (*to lynch, to boycott; colt, sandwich*). As a result of the commercial promotion of goods, trade marks are equally used as lexical words (*Kleenex, Walkman, to hoover*, etc.).

The shortening of words in various ways has become an increasingly productive pattern, not least because it enables us to concentrate on salient bits of information in an economical way. Thus it is not surprising that it is particularly frequent in administration and the media, but also in informal and rapid speech. In 'clipping' syllables are cut off from a word, as in *pub* <

public house, bike < bicycle. 'Blends' are formed from parts of existing words, such as *brunch* (< *breakfast + lunch*), *bit* (< *binary + digit*). Among the most productive patterns in present-day English are 'acronyms', i.e. full words formed from the initial letters of other words, such as *radar* (< *radio detecting and ranging*), *laser* (< *light amplification by the stimulated emission of radiation*) or *AIDS* (< *acquired immune deficiency syndrome*), and 'initialisms' such as *IBM, BBC,* in which the initials are still pronounced separately.

New words can also result from morphological **reanalysis**. Thus the nouns *editor* and *peddler/pedlar* were wrongly analysed as being derived from non-existent verbs, which were eventually formed, giving *to edit* and *to peddle.* This process of **back-formation** is evidently due to analogy with pairs like *teach/teacher,* etc. Similarly, some words ending in *-s* in the singular were reanalysed by speakers as plurals, and new singulars were formed: *cherry* (< Old French *cherise*), *pea < pease* (< Old English *pise,* late Latin *pisa*).

A famous case of morphological reanalysis is the story of *-burger.* Originally part of the proper name *Hamburger* 'relating to (the city of) Hamburg', it was reanalysed as English *ham* 'kind of meat' + *burger.* The latter has become productive as a suffix-like morpheme in combination with other similar types of food, as in *cheeseburger, vegeburger*; today *burger* can even be used as an independent word.

Changes of meaning

So far we have focused on the formal aspect of coining new words. But words and morphemes also change their meanings in various ways, a process which often mirrors the social context in which this happens. It is often claimed that 'every word has its own history', and dictionaries like the *Oxford English Dictionary* (for English) and the *Trésor de la langue française* (for French) offer a wealth of information on individual word histories. Nevertheless, we still do not know much about the general principles of meaning change. This is partly due to the enormous size of the vocabulary of many languages, with hundreds of thousands of words and many more individual word meanings, but it also reflects the long neglect of semantics, the science of meaning, within linguistics. Most existing classifications of semantic change are largely descriptive and based on various, partly overlapping criteria.

A basic distinction relates to the **extension** and **narrowing of meaning**. In the case of extension a word meaning becomes more general, as when English *bird*, which originally denoted only a 'young bird', developed to 'bird' (in general); this change can be described as the loss of the meaning component (or 'semantic feature') [+ young]. But meaning extension can also involve the development of an additional new word meaning. The main mechanism in this latter type of extension, and possibly in semantic change in general, is **metaphor**, which involves the transfer of a term because of an imagined similarity. Thus *neck* 'part of the body' was metaphorically extended to refer to anything resembling a neck such as a bottle neck; in a similar way most words for body parts have been metaphorically extended (cf. *head of state*, *foot of a mountain*, *heart of the organization*, etc.). **Metonymy**, another mechanism of extension, rests on physical contiguity and typically uses the name of an attribute to denote the whole entity, such as *White House* for the American president, *crown* for the king or queen, or place names for specific products, like *cognac*, *jersey*.

The inverse process of narrowing occurred, for example, in English *fowl*, where the original meaning 'bird' (in general) narrowed down to 'fowl', i.e. a specific kind of bird (cf. Old English *fugol* and the cognate German *Vogel*, both meaning 'bird'); similarly *meat*, originally 'food', as still preserved in *mincemeat*. Furthermore, words with multiple meanings, so-called polysemes, may lose a particular meaning in the course of time; see the discussion of *silly* below.

A particular type of semantic change, known as 'semantic bleaching', is connected with the process of **grammaticalization**, as when English *will* developed from its original full verb meaning 'to want' into the modern auxiliary *will*, which now only has grammatical meaning (cf. the discussion in Chapter 4).

Meanings have also been classified with regard to speaker evaluation, as neutral, positive, or negative, and such evaluations are also subject to change. This typically happens because of the associations words take in different uses or contexts, i.e. in the process of speech, but such associations or 'connotations' may in time become part of the systematic meaning of a word, its 'denotation'. This can be nicely illustrated by some English terms for the status and occupations of people. An improvement or **amelioration of meaning** has occurred in the case of *knight*, originally 'boy, youth, attendant', which had 'improved' by Middle English to its modern meaning. (The German cognate *Knecht* 'farm-hand' clearly developed in the opposite direction.) A negative evaluation or **pejoration of meaning** has developed in terms such as *knave* (< Old English *cnafa* 'boy, servant', cf. the cognate German *Knabe* 'boy'), *churl* (< Old English *ceorl* 'peasant, low-ranking freeman'), *villain* (< Middle English 'feudal serf'), which were once rather neutral terms for members of lower social ranks. Most of these examples mirror extra-linguistic social changes, i.e. the increasingly low status of certain social groups. In a similar way, many terms referring to women have undergone pejoration, while the corresponding terms for men have remained neutral or have improved, cf. *master* vs. *mistress*, *bachelor* vs. *spinster*—which again mirrors the traditional lower status of women in our society.

Extensive shifts of meaning often cloud the relationship between the original meaning and the modern one(s), as in English *silly* (< Old English *(ge)sælig* 'happy, blessed', as still preserved in its German cognate *selig*). A look at the intermediate stages, however, makes the development more transparent. From its original meaning attested till the late 15th century, *silly* passed through the following main stages: 'innocent' (late 13th c.–18th c.) > 'deserving pity' (c. 1300–19th c.) > 'weak, feeble' (13th c.– 19th c.), 'simple, ignorant' (16th c.–c. 1800), 'feeble-minded' (16th c.– today), 'foolish, empty-headed' (late 16th c.– today). These dates illustrate that typically an old meaning is not replaced immediately by a new one, but that both coexist for some time, each in specific contexts. A semantic change very similar to that of *silly* happened to French *crétin* 'stupid person', which, like French *chrétien* 'Christian', derives from Latin *christianus* 'Christian'. (See also Readings, Text 5.)

Why do word meanings change?

The above survey has been largely descriptive, though the discussion of metaphor, metonymy, and the social dimension of change in amelioration and pejoration has already touched upon some more general mechanisms. Let us now look at some further forces, both linguistic and extralinguistic, behind semantic change.

One of these is the need, mentioned at the beginning of this chapter, to adapt language to new communicative requirements. Apart from borrowing or coining new words, speakers frequently use existing words whose meanings are metaphorically or metonymically extended. Thus *torpedo* originally referred to a 'flat fish ... which emits electric rays', *tank* to a 'large container for holding liquids'; at least with *torpedo*, the new military meaning has become the primary one. When existing objects change their form but retain their basic function, the old word may, but need not, be retained as well. English *torch* has kept its original meaning, but now also refers to a 'small portable electric lamp', while German has formed the new compound *Taschenlampe*, literally 'pocket lamp' for the latter, but refers to the former as *Fackel*.

Another, psychological factor in semantic change is a basic human tendency to emphasize and exaggerate. Constant use of words may wear off their specific meaning, so that new, more expressive terms are sought. Thus we witness a constant change of English intensifying adverbs meaning 'very', from Old English *swiþe* to Middle English *full* and modern *very* (< Old French *verrai* 'true'), *really*, *extremely*, *awfully*.

A central psychological factor in lexical change is taboo, our tendency to avoid direct reference to unpleasant or socially stigmatized concepts such as death, old age, illness and sexuality. In tabooed fields speakers resort to the strategy of using euphemisms, i.e. neutral words for referring to stigmatized concepts, like *to pass away* for *to die*, or *to sleep with somebody*. But through frequent use the euphemistic word may itself come to be regarded as too explicit, so that new euphemistic terms are used. Tabooed fields themselves may also change. In many modern western societies, old age, it seems, has become taboo, leading to euphemisms like *senior citizens* and *the elderly*, while we have become increasingly explicit in sexual matters. In some societies the force of taboo is so strong that neither the name of a deceased person nor any word resembling this name may be used any longer. In such speech communities a constant and rapid turnover even of basic vocabulary takes place.

Apart from such extralinguistic factors, linguistic forces behind semantic change have been proposed, though they are less easy to prove.

Among these is the fact that the vocabulary of a language is not simply a list of formally more or less related words, but is also structured into groups of semantically related words, so-called semantic (or lexical) fields. The meaning relations between words seem to play a major role in semantic change, as the above discussion of the changes of *bird* and *fowl* has illustrated. These two words referring to birds changed their relative status as superordinate ('bird in general') and subordinate term ('specific kind of bird'). At least part of the vocabulary is structured in this way, such as verbs of motion, verbs of saying, etc. A meaning change of any member of a semantic field typically affects the (range of) meanings of the other members as well, and this also applies to changes in the field due to the addition or disappearance of a word.

It has frequently been observed that the borrowing of a word for which a synonymous native word exists either leads to the disappearance of one of the two or to their semantic differentiation (cf. above for *ceapman* vs. *merchant*). Thus the broad meaning of Old English *heofon* 'heaven and sky' narrowed down to 'heaven' as a result of the borrowing of Scandinavian *sky*, which originally meant 'cloud'. There seems to be a tendency for languages (or rather their speakers) to avoid synonymous words for reasons of economy. A related tendency is to reduce the extent of polysemy, i.e. the attachment of too many different meanings to a single word. Finally, when two words with similar or opposite meanings become homonyms, i.e. formally identical, this may lead to communicative difficulties, often referred to as 'homonymic clash'. Thus Old English *lætan* 'to let' and *lettan* 'to hinder' evidently had almost opposite meanings, but became homonyms under the form *let*. The gradual disappearance of the meaning 'to hinder' (which is still preserved in the phrase *without let or hindrance*) seems to be due to this clash. In general, however, homonyms are sufficiently disambiguated by the context for both forms to continue to exist side by side, cf. *meat/meet*, *waste/waist*.

The above discussion has identified a number of forces leading to semantic change, but we are still far from establishing more general principles of change in word meaning. (For a recent proposal, see Readings, Text 6.) With grammar we are on more secure ground, as we shall see in the following chapter.

4

Grammatical change

In the previous chapter we focused on changes in isolated words, with regard to both form and meaning. But speakers normally use words in utterances in which they are grammatically related to other words in a variety of ways. Both the inflection of words and the way in which words are arranged in an utterance provide communicatively important information on these grammatical relationships within an utterance. These grammatical devices are also subject to change in various ways.

Morphological change

In Chapter 3 we discussed morphemes as elements used for coining new words, such as the verbal base *teach* plus the suffix *-er* in *teacher*. But there is another type of morpheme which provides information on the grammatical relations between words within a sentence. Thus English *teach.es* can be analysed into the 'free' lexical morpheme *teach* and the 'bound' inflectional (or 'grammatical') morpheme *-es*, which expresses the rather complex meaning '3rd person singular present tense'. It is on such inflectional morphemes that this section will concentrate.

Languages may have very different types of morphological structure and these have formed the basis for various typological classifications. A widespread—though variously modified—**typology** groups languages into **isolating**, **agglutinating** and **inflecting**. In isolating languages like Chinese, words generally consist of single morphemes; in an agglutinating language like Turkish, words consist of more than one morpheme, but each morpheme is formally neatly separable and has a single meaning. In inflecting languages such as Latin or Greek, on the other hand, morpheme boundaries are frequently blurred, and several meanings may be compressed into one form; in Latin *am.as* 'you love', for example, the inflection *-as* carries the meanings '2nd person, singular, present, indicative' (cf. also the above analysis of *teaches*). Many languages, including English, do not fit neatly into one of these categories, but the classification still provides a useful descriptive framework for historical linguistics.

It has been claimed—though controversially—that languages tend to change their morphological type in a kind of cycle, with isolating languages becoming agglutinating, these in turn gradually becoming inflecting, only to end up as isolating again. Changes from isolating structures to agglutinating ones have been observed in pidgin and creole languages (cf. Chapter 6), where unstressed independent lexical and grammatical words have become prefixes and suffixes as a result of phonological reduction. English also has considerably changed its morphological structure since the time of its predominantly inflecting Proto-Germanic parent language. The reconstructed Proto-Germanic dative plural **dag.u.miz* 'to-the-days' consisted of three morphological elements, the root **dag-*, the so-called 'theme' *-u-* and the case inflection **-miz*. The latter two had fused into a single morpheme *-um* by the Old English period resulting in the form *dag.um*. Old English still had a system of four inflectional cases, similar to modern German, and only slightly simpler than Latin. Compare the plural inflection of the Old English word for 'days': nominative/accusative *dag.as*, genitive *dag.a*, dative *dag.um*. This system had largely collapsed by the early Middle English period, in particular because of the general weakening of unstressed vowels and the subsequent loss of unstressed final syllables.

As case endings disappeared in the Middle English period, the various functions of the inflected Old English cases (such as that of indirect object, or of adverb, etc.) were increasingly taken over by prepositional phrases with uninflected nouns. Modern English has lost most of its original inflections, not only on nouns but also on verbs, adjectives, and pronouns, thus changing from an inflecting **synthetic** to a predominantly **analytic language**, in which free grammatical words and fixed word order have taken over much of the former functions of inflections. A similar development has in many instances taken place between the highly inflected Latin and its Romance daughter languages like French or Italian; compare the Latin dative singular *amic.o* 'to-the-friend' with the functionally largely equivalent prepositional phrase French *à l'ami*, Italian *all' amico*, Spanish *al amigo*.

The above changes from inflectional to analytic involve the reduction of unstressed final vowels and syllables and are thus closely linked to sound changes (see Chapter 5). Let us now look at a more general mechanism of morphological change, which interacts with sound change in various ways, namely **analogy**. Analogical change occurs when one form adjusts to resemble another one with which it is related in form or meaning. Inflectional morphemes, for example, relate to each other in specific sets or 'paradigms' and there is a tendency to remove such irregularities in the patterns. Let us illustrate this with the two main types of analogy, 'proportional analogy' and 'analogical levelling'.

Proportional (or 'four-part') analogy rests on the application of the equation A:B :: C:X, i.e. 'A is to B as C is to What?'. This can be regarded as the basis of the analogical extension of the predominating Middle English plural forms of nouns in -(*e*)*s* to the still substantial number of Middle English irregular plurals like *kine* 'cows', *eyen* 'eyes', *word* 'words', etc.; here the equation would be '*bull* : *bulls* :: *cow* : X', with X being interpreted as *cows* instead of original *kine*.

An example of the second type, analogical levelling, is provided by a number of Old English strong ('irregular') verbs. These had four different but formally and semantically related forms (against the three of modern English), such as *freosan–freas–fruron–froren* 'freeze–froze–frozen'. With Old English *freosan* the stem-final consonant alternated between *s* and *r* as the result of a regular sound change of the original [s] > [r] in the last two forms. However, such consonantal alternation only existed in a small number of verbs, while the majority had the same stemfinal consonant in all four forms. Accordingly one of the two variants of the verb stem was by analogy adapted to the other one in its stem-final consonant, resulting in the uniform modern English pattern *freeze–froze–frozen*. (Old High German had the same consonantal alternation as Old English, but it generalized the [r] in all forms, cf. modern German *frieren–fror–gefroren*.) This example also illustrates the general fact that regular sound change may lead to irregularities in morphological patterns, which may be made morphologically regular again by the working of analogy.

There have been some attempts to discover general rules for morphological analogy, but these are at best tendencies for which numerous counter-examples can be found. Thus it seems that basic forms influence derived forms, rather than the other way round, and that double morphological marking tends to replace single marking rather than vice versa. An example of the tendency for double marking is provided by German *Baum* 'tree'; its original plural *Baume* (marked only by the plural suffix *-e*) was replaced by a new, doubly marked plural *Bäume* in analogy to *Gast–Gäste* 'guest(s)', where such double marking by vowel alternation and the suffix *-e* was the regular development.

So far we have described some morphological changes and looked at a major mechanism of such changes, namely analogy. But neither descriptions of changes nor the establishing of rules or tendencies of analogy offer any explanation for *why* these changes occur. We still need a more general principle behind these mechanisms. A promising answer to this question may be provided by the concept of 'naturalness'. Some morphological forms seem to be more natural (or 'unmarked'), which implies not only that they are more frequent, but also that they are internalized early in child language acquisition, are more resistant to change (though they often result from change), and are typical of pidgin and creole languages (cf. Chapter 6). Furthermore, naturalness follows some general principles such as that of 'constructional iconicity', i.e. the principle that the *semantically* more complex form is also *morphologically* more complex. Thus the notion of plurality is semantically 'more' than that of 'singularity', so it is to be expected that a plural is also morphologically 'more' than a singular, i.e. that something is added to express a plural. This principle has empirical support since the languages of the world typically have morphological plural marking, while marked singulars are extremely rare. It has been claimed that morphological change proceeds towards more natural forms. Thus, the English plural *words* is more natural than the original Old English plural *word*, which violated the principle of constructional iconicity since it was formally identical with the singular. Though there are still English plurals that do not conform to this principle (*sheep*, *fish*, etc.), a very large number of similar non-iconic plurals have become iconic in the history of English. Obviously, some of these changes can equally be explained as due to analogy, but the theory of natural morphology claims—though not un-controversially—to provide a more comprehensive and possibly universal framework for a wide range of morphological changes. (For a critical view on naturalness see Readings, Text 8.)

Syntactic change

After a period of relative neglect, syntactic change has become the focus of much research in the last three decades, though there is still no generally accepted theoretical framework for its study.

If we look at the history of a particular language such as English, we can notice a great number of syntactic changes from Old English to the present time. Old English only knew two tenses, a present and a past tense, and the modern opposition between the simple and the so-called 'progressive' forms, as in *I read* vs. *I am reading*, was still not fully established by Shake-speare's time (you may remember Polonius asking Hamlet, who is absorbed in a book, 'What do you read, my lord?'). Similarly, negations and questions could still be formed without the use of *do* in Shakespeare's time: thus *I know not* or *Whom trust you more*, the latter with inversion of verb and subject. As with lexical and morphological changes, such individual develop-ments are certainly interesting in their own right, but here again linguists have been trying to discover more general and abstract principles of syntactic change.

In the following section a few of these central issues will be briefly discussed, starting with two important mechanisms of syntactic change, namely the reanalysis of surface structures and the process of **grammaticalization**—though not every syntactic change can be accounted for in this way. The ensuing discussion of some typological aspects of syntactic change will link the question of syntactic change to more general typological properties of languages.

Reanalysis. Syntactic constructions may be or become ambiguous in specific contexts and speakers may come to favour a new analysis rather than the old one in the course of time. In general the two analyses will coexist for some time, till the new one may finally replace the old one and may subsequently even be extended to similar constructions. The reanalysis of a given surface structure (which we also met in some vocabulary change, see Chapter 3) is a major mechanism behind syntactic change. English offers some interesting examples in which the gradual disappearance of inflections, i.e. a morphological factor, has led to such a reanalysis, while the inflected German language has preserved the original structure.

Consider the following German sentence and its often-quoted Old English equivalent, to which a literal translation and a syntactic analysis (identical for both sentences) is added:

Dem König gefielen die Birnen
Đæm cyninge licodon peran.

'To-the-king pleased (the)pears.'
O (dat. sing.)–V (past plur.)–S (nom. plur.)

In the two sentences, the noun phrases *Dem König* and *Đæm cyninge* 'To-the-king' are indirect objects in the dative case, while the subjects are the nominative nouns *Birnen* and *peran*. The extensive loss of inflections in Middle English, however, resulted in the uninflected form *the king*, which was formally identical for both subject and object. Owing to the loss of the verbal plural marking -*on* by the late Middle English period, verb forms such as *liked* equally had become unmarked for number and person. The resulting construction *The king liked pears* now allows for two different syntactic analyses, since each of the two nouns may be interpreted as grammatical S(ubject) or O(bject), i.e. *The king* (S/O?) *liked* (singular/plural?) *(the) pears* (S/O?), with the overall sentence meaning remaining more or less the same with both interpretations (in spite of a slight semantic change of the verb cf. 'The king liked the pears' vs. 'The pears pleased (to) the king') The predominating unmarked Middle English word order Subject–Verb–Object (SVO) led to the reanalysis of *the king* a subject, though the old analysis of *the king* as object was still supported by the personal pronouns (*he* vs. *him*) and survived with some verbs into the sixteenth century.

Grammaticalization. This second mechanism of syntactic change is more complex than reanalysis. As the term implies, in grammaticalization originally lexical words increasingly adopt a grammatical function, a process which often combines a semantic change of the word in question ('semantic bleaching', see Chapter 3), its phonetic reduction, and a reanalysis of the original form. In extreme cases this may result in the change of a free lexical morpheme into a bound grammatical morpheme, such as a suffix. Thus grammaticalization can affect both morphology and syntax, and furthermore involves changes on the phonological and semantic levels as well. The phenomenon itself has been known for a long time, but has attracted considerable attention recently.

Some frequent kinds of grammaticalization also attested in English are: (i) development from main to auxiliary verbs (e.g. English *will*, which originally meant 'want', as German *Ich will* 'I want (to)' still does); (ii) development of the progressive form from a construction consisting of a 'particle of place + non-finite verb' (cf. English *he is hunting* < *he is a-hunting* < *is on hunting*); (iii) development of negative particles from negative intensifiers such as French *ne … pas* 'not … a step', or English *not*, *nought* and German *nicht*, which go back to *nowiht*, *niwiht*, originally meaning 'not a thing'.

The expression of future provides a good example of grammaticalization in various languages, including English. The original English full verb *will* 'want' developed into an auxiliary marking the future; in this function it can be contracted to *'ll*, thus being subject to both semantic bleaching and phonological reduction. Similarly, the English *going to* future developed from a construction with the full verb of motion *go*, which was reanalysed from expressing actual movement (*I am going to the shop*) to intended (or future) action (*I am going to collect my things from the shop, I am going to phone/fly to London tonight*). Though full grammaticalization of this construction only happened in the early nineteenth century, it has expanded rapidly, with a possible phonetic reduction to *gonna*. The emergence of a new functional category for referring to future events has evidently affected the already existing category, since the new form refers to events which are going to happen with some certainty in the immediate future. A similar development of a *going to* future is also found with French *aller* 'go' (cf. *Mon père va arriver dans quelques instants* 'My father is going to arrive in a few moments') and in a number of other languages. (For grammaticalization see also Readings, Text 7.)

Typology and implicational changes. In reanalysis and grammaticalization a number of factors and linguistic levels interact in bringing about a particular change. Let us look finally at syntactic changes which show an implicational relation to other changes, i.e. which seem to trigger off specific further changes. This has been most clearly documented in changes connected with syntactic typologies, i.e. the classification of languages on the basis of certain syntactic features.

The typological classification where these implicational relations become most evident is the one based on the basic, unmarked word order of the main sentence constituents S(ubject)–V(erb)–O(bject). Of the six possible arrangements of these three categories, the patterns SVO (as in most European languages including English) and SOV (as in Basque, Turkish, Japanese) are the most widespread ones, followed by VSO (Welsh, classical Arabic, early Hebrew). In the 1960s, Joseph Greenberg established a number of so-called implicational syntactic universals, i.e. certain correspondences between the relative order of V and O on the one hand and a number of syntactic patterns on the other, and these have been used successfully—though not uncontroversially—for describing and explaining syntactic change. Languages with the basic order VO share certain other word order patterns and grammatical features, which tend to have precisely the opposite value in OV languages. In VO languages, for example, not only do verbs precede objects, but auxiliaries precede main verbs, and comparative adjectives precede the noun (*harder than stone*) as do *pre*positions (*from him*). Languages with OV order, i.e. with verb-final position, however, have the reverse order in all these patterns, including *post*positions (*him from*), at least in normal or 'unmarked' constructions. The diachronic relevance of these correspondences lies in the observation that a language which changes its basic order from VO to OV or vice versa also seems to change all or most of the above other characteristics accordingly. Thus, Proto-Indo-European has been reconstructed as an originally rather consistent OV language by way of comparative reconstruction. In the oldest Germanic texts, including Old English, we still find occasional OV patterns such as postpositions (e.g. Old English *þa þe him from noldon* 'who did not want (to go) from him') and OV comparative patterns, especially in the conservative language of poetry. These relics of a former OV stage were increasingly replaced by VO patterns in later texts.

There are various possible reasons for such profound syntactic change. Apart from contact with other languages (see Chapter 6), discourse factors may play a role; thus, originally stylistically marked word orders (emphasis, topicalization) may become unmarked through frequent use. Such a shift in the markedness value of particular constructions is rather easy in inflected languages, where word order is more flexible, since the grammatical relations within the sentence are sufficiently indicated by inflections. (For a cross-linguistic approach to historical syntax see Readings, Text 9; for shift of markedness see also Text 10.)

Our discussion of linguistic change has so far dealt with morphemes and words as well as with combinations of these; here specific meanings are attached to specific forms, and evidently both the form and the meaning are liable to change. But more basically, all linguistic elements of a language are built from discrete sound units, each of which may be subject to change as well. The following chapter will provide a more systematic discussion of how the sounds of a language can change.

5
Sound change

The study of sound change is the best researched area of historical linguistics, with the longest tradition. The relatively small number and systematic structure of distinctive sounds make them more easily accessible to linguistic analysis on both the synchronic and the diachronic level. The speech sounds we hear are realizations or 'allophones' of underlying abstract distinctive sound units, the **phonemes**. Sound change or **phonological change** may happen both on the concrete level of speech production (**phonetic change**) and on the abstract level of phonemes (**phonemic change**). Though there is some relation between these two types of change, they are neither identical nor directly linked.

How sounds are produced

We can only understand phonetic change if we know the basic principles of how speech sounds are produced. In the production of vowels and consonants, the speaker modifies the airflow from the lungs through different positions and movements of the speech organs, i.e. the vocal folds, larynx, oral and nasal cavities, tongue, jaws, teeth and lips. The involvement of speech organs, as well as acoustic criteria, provide the basis for a classification of sounds.

All vowels are voiced sounds, i.e. the passing airflow is modified by the vibrating vocal folds or cords. The quality of vowels results from the shape of the oral cavity, which depends mainly on the position of the tongue, though lips and jaws also play some role. A rather low tongue produces the 'open' or 'low' vowel [a], while the tongue is raised for the 'closed' or 'high' vowels [i, u]. With 'front' or 'palatal' vowels the front part of the tongue is raised, with 'back' or 'velar' ones its back part, with central vowels being in the middle. On the basis of the position of the tongue in the mouth vowels can be represented in the following diagram, where the vowels on the left side are front vowels, those on the right side back vowels.

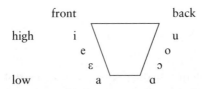

Some consonants such as [z, v, ð, ʒ, dʒ], i.e. the initial consonants in *zeal*, *veal*, *this*, *genre*, *Jim*, are also voiced, while others are voiceless and lack this vibration, such as initial [s, f, θ, ʃ, tʃ] in *sat*, *fat*, *thing*, *ship*, *chat*. The production of all consonants involves different kinds of obstruction of the airflow (called 'manner of articulation'): with stops like [p, t, k, b, d, g] the air is briefly blocked, while fricatives (or 'spirants') like [f, s, θ, ʃ, v, z, ð, ʒ] have a substantial obstruction of the airflow; affricates such as [tʃ, dʒ] (*chin*, *gin*) result from the release of air from the position of a stop into that of a fricative. Another parameter for classification is the place of articulation, i.e. the point where the obstruction is formed: the labials [p, b] involve the lips, the labiodentals [f, v] the teeth and lower lips. [θ, ð] are formed with the tongue against the teeth, while [s, z, ʃ, ʒ] involve different parts of the alveolar ridge just behind the teeth; with nasal consonants the nasal cavity serves as a resonator, producing bilabial [m], dental or alveolar [n], and velar [ŋ] as in *sing*.

Phonetic change

Sound change takes place when any of the parameters discussed in the previous section changes in the production of vowels and consonants, often under the influence of neighbouring sounds. The form and movement of the speech organs in sound production make certain changes more likely (or 'natural') than others, which is borne out by the description of a vast number of sound changes in the languages of the world. Of the various processes involved, the following are among the most important.

The **palatalization** of vowels, i.e. the 'fronting' of the raised part of the tongue towards the palate as in the change from [u] > [y] (the sound in French *une*, or German *Glück*), or of [o] > [e], was frequent in the development of pre-Old English. It is still reflected in the vowel alternation of pairs such as English *mouse–mice*, *foot–feet*, etc., where the vowel in the second forms was palatalized by an [i] which originally followed in the next syllable; thus pre-Old English *[muːsi-] > Old English [myːs] 'mice', *[foːti-] > [feːt] 'feet'. In **velarization**, on the other hand, the tongue moves back towards the velum or soft palate. This accounts for the difference in the vowel sounds between English *sword* and German *Schwert* [e], which both go back to a common Germanic form with [e], velarized in Old English to [o]. Vowels may also be raised, as in English *goose*, *boot*, where [uː] developed from Middle English [oː]; or they may be lowered, i.e. become more open, as frequently happens before [r]. Other vocalic changes involve the degree of lip rounding. Thus the rounded vowel [yː] in Old English *mȳs* was subsequently unrounded to [iː], as is still reflected in the modern English spelling *mice*. Furthermore, oral or 'pure' vowels may become nasalized as in French, which has developed a whole series of nasal vowels before nasal consonants, cf. *fin* [ɛ̃]'end', *an* [ã] 'year', etc.

Diphthongization changes a simple vowel into a diphthong, i.e. a vowel in whose production the tongue changes its position, as in English *house*, *ride*, which in Middle English had [uː] and [iː] respectively; on the other hand, in some British English varieties we increasingly hear **monophthongization** (or 'levelling') of diphthongs before [ə] as in *fire*, *tower*, even resulting in [faː], [tɑː].

Consonants may change both their manner and their place of articulation. A widespread change in manner of articulation is **spirantization**, the change from stop to fricative ('spirant'), as in Grimm's Law, when the Indo-European voiceless stops [p, t, k] became voiceless fricatives [f, θ, x] in the Germanic languages (see Chapter 2). In the change [p] > [f] spirantization is combined with an additional change from a bilabial articulation, i.e. one involving both lips, to a labiodental one involving lip and teeth. But stops can also develop into affricates, as in the change of pre-

Old English [k] > [tʃ] before palatal vowels in words like *child*, *church*, a change also subsumed under palatalization.

Phonetic change may be **unconditioned**, i.e. affect all occurrences of a specific sound irrespective of its context. More frequently, however, it is **conditioned** in that it only occurs in a specific phonetic environment, as when in English [r] was lost before consonants and word-finally, as in *court* [kɔːt], *hair* [heə], but was retained in all other positions, cf. *ring* [rɪŋ], *hairy* [heəri], etc.

So far we have described various types of frequent sound changes. Even more important than the description of such individual sound changes, however, is the establishment of more general types of sound change including groups or clusters of sounds. This will make some phonological processes more transparent and will help us to understand better the nature of these changes.

Lenition is a cover term for various processes which involve some 'weakening' of sounds (though the term is not well defined); lenition processes involve, in some kind of hierarchical order, (i) voicing, i.e. the change of voiceless consonants to voiced ones as frequently happens between vowels, cf. Latin intervocalic [p, t, k] > Spanish [b, d, g], as in *pagado* 'pacified, pleased' (< Latin *pacatum*); (ii) spirantization (cf. Grimm's Law above and see Chapter 2); (iii) vocalization of consonants, as in French *paume* 'palm' (< Latin *palma*) or the Cockney pronunciation of English *milk* as [mɪʊk]; (iv) the **deletion** or disappearance of sounds, as in French *mûr* 'mature' (< Latin *maturus*).

There are different types of sound deletion and the opposite process of sound insertion, all with specific technical terms. The most important ones are: apocope, i.e. word-final vowel loss, as in many English words still written with -*e*, which was pronounced well into the Middle English period, such as Middle English *nose* [nɔːsə], *tale* [taːlə], etc.; syncope, the deletion of an unstressed medial vowel, as in *every* [evri], and frequently as an informal variant of English words like [hɪstri] *history*; epenthesis, the insertion of a vowel or consonant, as in Japanese *futoboro* 'football', or English *thimble* < Old English *þymel*, but also often heard in the pronunciation of *prince* as *prints* [prɪnts] or *film* as [fɪləm].

Many changes result from the mutual influence and contact between segments in the process of speech production. Our impression of hearing the discrete sounds [l] [ɪ] [p] [s] in the pronunciation of *lips* results from the working of our brain and our knowledge of the language, but does not correspond to the acoustic reality. When we speak, our speech organs do not jump from one position to the next, but are in continuous movement. What is of interest here is that this continuous movement of the speech organs may lead to a partial anticipation of the position of a following sound, or the continuation of a preceding one into the next, which often increases the ease of articulation. This is the process that brings about one of the most widespread types of change, namely **assimilation**, the partial or total adjustment of a sound to another one. The term itself illustrates the process nicely, since Latin *assimilare* derives through assimilation from *ad + similis* 'like'. In the first syllables of English *im.possible*, *il.literate* the two different allomorphs of a morpheme meaning 'not' are due to assimilation to the following consonant, while the unassimilated form is seen in *in.correct*. Assimilation is the reason for the nasalization of vowels next to nasal consonants as in French *fin* [fɛ̃] 'end', and also for the fronting in *mice*, *feet* before the originally following [i] that we noted above. All these changes have been fully implemented in the language and have been ratified in encoded forms. But there are many more assimilations which only occur in rapid speech, such as *quite good* pronounced as [kwaɪ(k) ɡʊd]. Some of these may also one day become part of the linguistic system, while others will remain restricted to individual utterances; here we see again the correlation between performance-related changes and changes which become generalized and enter the underlying abstract system of a language, a phenomenon we have come across before. Assimilation may be both regressive or progressive, i.e. work backwards or forwards.

Much rarer is **dissimilation**, whereby two identical or similar sounds become less similar, e.g. English *pilgrim* < Latin *peregrinus*, or German *Kartoffel* 'potato', replacing original *tartoffel*.

The changes discussed so far all relate to changes in the quality of sounds, but there are equally changes in quantity, i.e. in the length of segments, particularly of vowels. Vowel shortening frequently happens before consonant clusters, in words with three or more syllables, and in unstressed position; it accounts for the vowel alternation in pairs such as *keep/kept*, *holy/holiday* (which originally had the same long vowel in both members of each pair), and for the short vowel in English *us*, which had Old English [uː]. Lengthening often occurs in open syllables, i.e. those ending in a vowel, as in *nose*, *tale*, pronounced in Middle English [nɔːsə], [taːlə], and before certain consonant groups, as in *find*, which had a short vowel in Old English. **Compensatory lengthening** tends to go hand in hand with the deletion of a consonant after a short vowel, when an originally short vowel becomes long. This keeps the overall length of the syllable constant, since the total quantity of a short vowel plus a consonant equals that of a long vowel in phonological terms. This process is reflected in the cognate pair English *goose* and German *Gans* 'goose' (< Germanic **gans-*), where the English long vowel is due to compensatory lengthening after the loss of [n], while German has kept the original short vowel and the nasal consonant.

Phonemic change

A discussion of phonetic changes like that in the previous section is certainly interesting, particularly for the history of individual words, but it tells us nothing about systemic changes, i.e. changes in the abstract phonemic system of a particular language.

Languages differ in their number of phonemes and in the way these are organized into systems, and both these dimensions may also be subject to change. Thus classical Latin had a system of five long and five short vowels, while modern Italian as one of its daughter languages has a seven-vowel system without quantity opposition; both phonological systems, however, consist only of pure, i.e. non-nasalized vowels, which can be arranged in a triangular pattern along the dimensions of front–back and open–closed. French, another daughter language of Latin, has developed a new type of nasal vowels as in *un* 'one', *bon* 'good' beside the original pure vowels, thereby profoundly changing its overall vowel system through the introduction of a new opposition between pure and nasal vowels. As far as consonants are concerned, modern English has clearly more fricatives than stops, while its Indo-European parent had few fricatives but a considerable number of stops including aspirated ones (cf. the discussion of Grimm's Law in Chapter 2).

By way of example, let us now look at the two main types of change in phonemic systems, namely **phonemic merger** and **phonemic split**.

A case of complete merger of two formerly distinct phonemes occurred with the two Middle English long *e* sounds, open /ɛː/ as in *meat*, *read*, and closed /eː/ as in *meet*, *reed*. (Slashes like '//' indicate phonemes, while square brackets refer to the realization of phonemes, i.e. to actual pronunciations.) These two vowels must have been similar in acoustic and articulatory terms, so that the 'margin of security' between them was rather small—a fact which may have contributed to their merging under /iː/ in Modern English. The corresponding velar pair of long *o* sounds, Middle English /oː/ as in *boot*, *moon* and /ɔː/ as in *boat*, *moan*, however, did not merge but underwent a shift to /uː/ and /oː/ respectively, thus increasing the phonetic space between the two phonemes, even more so by the later change from [oː] > [oʊ] > [əʊ] in *boat*, etc. in British standard English. Phonemic split, on the other hand, is typically connected with the development of different allophones in specific environments. Examples are provided by the above-mentioned irregular English plurals *feet*, *geese*, *mice*, etc., which in pre-Old English formed their nominative plural with the suffix *-iz*, thus singular */muːs-/, */foːt-/, plural */muːsiz/, */foːtiz/. The palatalization of the stem vowels before the following palatal [i] (see preceding section) yielded new rounded front vowels as in *[myːsiz], *[føːtiz], while they remained unchanged in other positions. This restriction of [yː], [øː] to the position before a following [i] means that they were still allophones of the phonemes /uː/ and /oː/. A phonemic transcription at that stage would thus still have to be */muːsiz/, */foːtiz/, even though the actual pronunciation of the forms showed [yː], [øː]. However, when the unstressed plural suffix *-iz* disappeared in the course of time, the occurrence of [uː] and [oː], as against [yː] and [øː] (later unrounded to [iː] and [eː]) was no longer predictable from the context; furthermore, the different meanings (i.e. singular vs. plural) of the Old English forms *mūs* vs. *mȳs*, *fōt* vs. *fēt* now only rested upon the opposition between the different stem vowels. This is the point where a split of the original two phonemes /uː/, /oː/ to the four phonemes /uː/, /yː/, /oː/, /øː/ has occurred, though no further *phonetic* change of the vowels is involved at this final stage. As the above discussion has shown, phonetic change may result in phonemic change, though this is by no means always the case; on the other hand, phonemic change may equally take place without an immediate phonetic change of the involved segment. Phonemic splits and mergers often interact in various ways, as when one of a set of newly split phonemes merges with an already existing one.

Since the phonemes of a language form a structured system, each individual phonemic change affects the whole. Some changes even trigger off a series of interrelated changes, so-called **chain shifts**. Depending on the beginning and direction of such chain shifts, we can distinguish between 'push chains' and 'drag chains'. Grimm's Law, the change of Indo-European /p, t, k/ > /f, θ, x/; /b, d, g/ > /p, t, k/; /bh, dh, gh/ > /b, d, g/ (cf. Chapter 2) is a famous case in point. The above three sets of changes are obviously interrelated, though their relative chronology is uncertain. A push chain account of Grimm's Law would see the beginning of the change with the shift /bh, dh, gh/ > /b, d, g/; in order to avoid mergers with the already existing set of /b, d, g/, the latter would develop to /p, t, k/, thus in turn pushing the existing /p, t, k/ to become fricatives. A drag chain account, on the other hand, sees the beginning of the change in the change of /p, t, k/ > /f, θ, x/, which would have left the positions of the voiceless stops empty. The resulting gap would have triggered off the devoicing of original /b, d, g/ in a kind of pull mechanism, leading to a new set of voiceless stops /p, t, k/, which in turn left empty the slot of voiced stops, into which the originally aspirated voiced stops were dragged.

Another famous chain shift for which both types of chain mechanisms as well as a combination of the two have been proposed is the English *Great Vowel Shift*. This shift of the whole system of Middle English long vowels involves a raising of each of the long vowels, thus /ɛː/ > /eː/ > /iː/ (*meat*), /eː/ > /iː/ (*meet*), etc (see above), except for the highest vowels /iː/ and /uː/, which were diphthongized leading to modern English /aɪ/, /aʊ/ (*mice*, *house* (see the simplified diagram below).

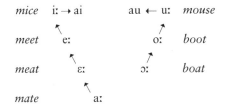

So far we have described phonemic change as a change of phonemic segments. However, we can also describe phonemes as bundles of distinctive phonological features, such as [voiced], [stop], [labial], [back], etc. A description of change in terms of specific features and rules for changing these in specific ways is not only more economical, but also helps to uncover more general tendencies which apply to whole classes of phonemes. Thus the three changes of Grimm's Law /p/ > /f/, /t/ > /θ/, /k/ > /x/ can more economically be described as a single change of the feature [– continuant] > [+ continuant], i.e. of stops to fricatives. (For a discussion of sound change in terms of phonological rules, see Readings, Text 11; for the influence of 'prosodic features', see Text 12.)

As some of the above examples illustrate, phonological change not only affects the shape of individual words and morphemes, but may also lead to a synchronic alternation in the realization of a specific morpheme, i.e. to different allomorphs, as in *mouse–mice*, or *divine–divinity*. From a synchronic point of view, such cases of so-called 'morphophonemic alternation' are part of the morphology of modern English; from a historical point of view, however, these alternations are the result of phonological changes, a fact which demonstrates the interaction of phonology and morphology in linguistic change.

6

Language contact

One of the main reasons why languages change is that they come into contact with other languages. This contact typically involves bilingual speakers, i.e. people who speak the two (or more) languages involved, at least to a certain extent. The languages of such individuals may act upon and influence each other in a wide range of ways: in the adoption of features of pronunciation, the borrowing of words, or the modification of grammar. From a purely linguistic point of view, language contact phenomena are neither good nor bad, but the attitude of speakers to such phenomena is frequently not as neutral (cf. Chapter 1). Since languages and speakers in contact are rarely of equal political, economic or social status and power, the less powerful or prestigious group is frequently disadvantaged. This often leads to language conflict between the speech communities.

Borrowing from other languages

The most frequent and obvious instances of linguistic borrowing are loan words, which enter a language as a result of various political and cultural factors. As discussed in Chapter 3, English started out with a predominantly Germanic vocabulary, but has integrated a huge number of loans in the course of its turbulent history. Similarly, the vocabulary of Romanian, which ultimately developed from Vulgar Latin, has become strongly influenced by Slavic, though Romanian has kept a basically Romance grammar. Such widespread replacement of native vocabulary has occurred in numerous languages of the world.

Lexical borrowing is often triggered by a perceived gap in the vocabulary of the recipient language, particularly with respect to cultural phenomena associated with the source or donor language. Well-known examples of such cultural borrowings in English are *thug* (from Hindi), *sherry* (from Spanish), *waltz* (from German), *ski* (from Norwegian), *sauna* (from Finnish) and, more recently, *glasnost* (from Russian) and *sushi* (from Japanese). This kind of cultural borrowing is abundantly evident in other languages as well, and seems to have greatly increased in modern times with developments in communication.

However, speakers may feel the need for borrowing not because their own language does not have a word for a particular object or concept, but because they think that the equivalent word in the donor language is somehow better or more prestigious. Many indigenous languages in former colonies have adopted large numbers of loans from the formerly more prestigious colonial languages such as French or English. Finnish has borrowed extensively from Germanic and Baltic languages even in such central fields as kinship terms and body parts (e.g. the terms for 'mother', 'daughter', 'sister', 'tooth', 'neck', etc.), though it had corresponding native terms. Loan words can also reflect the predominance of different languages in specific domains of use at particular periods of time. This accounts for the prevalence of French loans in English in such fields as the law (*crime*, *judge*), warfare (*officer*, *enemy*), government and administration (*reign*, *court*), fashion and food (*mirror*, *mutton*). And, as a glance at a fashion magazine or menu will reveal, French still provides English speakers with much of the vocabulary of *haute couture* and *haute cuisine*.

One influence on the extent of borrowing, then, is the perceived prestige of the donor language. Other factors are the length of language contact, the extent of the communication between different speech communities, and the number and status of their bilingual speakers. Borrowing also varies across different word classes. Nouns tend to be the most frequent followed by adjectives and verbs. It would appear that it is mainly in the naming of objects rather than attributes or processes that people find most deficiencies in their own languages. Pronoun and conjunctions, on the other hand, form closed sets of word and are therefore only rarely borrowed. But even within these word classes borrowing does occur, as the Scandinavian loans *they*, *their*, and *till* in Middle English illustrate.

Loan words tend to be adapted in varying degrees to the target language, especially if the two languages differ substantially in their phonologies and morphologies. Finnish, for example, does not have initial consonant clusters, so that Germanic *stranð* 'shore' (cf. German *Strand*) has been borrowed into Finnish as *ranta*. Japanese has mainly open syllables, i.e. syllables of the form 'consonant + vowel' (CV), so that English words with closed syllables, i.e. with the structure (C)VC(C) are restructured to fit into the Japanese phonological system, giving, for instance, *futoboro* 'football', *besuboru* 'baseball'.

Lexical borrowings can be subclassified in different ways according to the degree of formal adherence to the foreign model. While loan words are both semantically and formally borrowed from the source language, there are also different kinds of loan translations, i.e. more or less literal translations of complex foreign words into the target language; French *gratte-ciel* and German *Wolkenkratzer*, for example, are loan translations from English *skyscraper*.

Massive borrowing may substantially change the lexical structure of the target language. For example, only the first of the following six English verbs of thinking is Germanic and goes back to the Old English period, while the others are from French ('F') or Latin ('L'), and were introduced only from the fourteenth century onwards, providing the language with a number of stylistically differentiated near-synonyms: *think*; *reflect* (F/L, 15th c.); *meditate* (L, 16th c.); *ponder* (F, 14th c.); *consider* (F, 14th c.); *cogitate* (L, 16th c.).

Less obvious than lexical borrowing is structural borrowing, i.e. borrowing on the phonological, morphological, or syntactic levels. Some additions to the English phoneme inventory, such as the voiced fricatives /v, z, ʒ/ in words like *very*, *zeal*, *measure*, were obviously backed by the enormous intake of French words with these consonants, though native factors have also played some role. There are a number of syntactic constructions in English which are claimed to be due to structural borrowing, such as the 'progressive' form (*I am writing*) from Latin, and the 'empty' *do* in questions and negations from Celtic, though these claims are controversial (see also Readings, Text 13). Changes of the basic word order SVO as discussed in Chapter 4 may also be due to structural borrowing from neighbouring languages and language families.

Extensive structural borrowing on the different linguistic levels can result in linguistic **convergence**, i.e. in increased structural similarity even of genetically unrelated languages.

Convergence and linguistic areas

In situations of long and rather stable language contact, bilingual speakers tend to make their languages structurally more similar to ease communication and the acquisition of the other language(s). Unlike the piecemeal process of borrowing, this mutual convergence of different linguistic systems typically involves languages of similar social status, and brings about changes in all the languages involved. A famous case of mutual convergence is found in the multilingual Indian village of Kupwar, where two Indo-Aryan languages, Urdu and Marathi, and one unrelated Dravidian language, Kannada, are spoken by ethnically and socially different groups. Practically all inhabitants have known and used all three languages in their daily communication with members of the other groups over several centuries. As a result, the originally very different grammatical structures of the three languages have converged to such a high degree in Kupwar that they are now largely identical. On the other hand, the vocabularies of these languages have remained largely different, guaranteeing the linguistic independence of the speech communities.

Linguistic convergence may also occur over extended geographical areas and involve larger numbers of genetically related and unrelated languages, though it may be restricted to a number of linguistic features. Such **linguistic areas** have been found in India, Africa, the north-west coast of North America, etc. The most famous linguistic area is formed by a number of Balkan languages belonging to different language families or branches, such as Albanian, Slavic (varieties of Bulgarian, Macedonian, and to some extent Serbian), Romance (Romanian), and Greek. These languages share a great deal of vocabulary and a number of grammatical features, for example the placement of the definite article after the noun, the replacement of the infinitive by a different construction, and the specific formation of the numerals from 11 to 19 of the type 'one on ten'. The number and combination of these features vary for the individual Balkan languages, but the important point is that these shared 'Balkanisms' often do not occur in other members of the same language families or even in the same languages spoken outside the Balkan linguistic area. The source of a particular feature is often not clear, but it has been claimed that a language will only adopt features which correspond to a basic developmental tendency in the recipient language.

In Chapter 2 we saw how the family tree model tries to account for the rise of new languages from a common parent or proto-language. (For a further explanation see Readings, Text 14.) However, the family tree model cannot account for the fundamental changes which languages may undergo through close language contact. In some cases heavy borrowing and structural convergence have changed a language to such an extent that a genetic relation to parent and sister languages is no longer clear. Genetic relationship is particularly problematic in the case of the two types of contact languages discussed in the next section.

Language birth: pidgins and creoles

In the previous section we saw how languages in contact may become structurally more similar while still remaining separate languages. Under particular circumstances, however, intensive language contact may result in the birth of new types of contact languages, **pidgins** and **creoles**. A pidgin is an auxiliary language with a reduced structure and lexicon which develops to meet the communicative requirements of speakers of mutually unintelligible languages, mainly for certain rudimentary transactions in trade, seafaring, or the management of labour in general. This language expediently brings together the elements of the two disparate languages to the extent necessary to fulfil its restricted range of functions, most of which have to do with recurring and predictable situations in the here and now. A pidgin therefore has a highly elementary grammar and vocabulary designed to make as economical a connection with context as possible. A creole, on the other hand, is usually defined as a pidgin which has been adopted as a first language by a speech community and which has therefore developed in complexity to account for the much wider range of functions that a language needs to fulfil across a variety of domains of use in the maintenance of social life.

The study of pidgins and creoles reveals with particular clarity the processes of language change through contact. The speed in which the structural and lexical complexity of creoles tends to develop makes certain linguistic changes directly observable for linguists, while similar changes take much longer in other languages. Furthermore, there is an increasing awareness among linguists that some or even many of our modern languages may ultimately go back to former creoles which have developed into fully fledged languages without a trace of their ancestry. This hypothesis challenges the traditional view of linguistic evolution from proto-languages as discussed in Chapter 2, though some linguists have tried to apply the comparative method even to pidgin and creole languages to arrive at proto-pidgins.

We have every reason to assume that pidginization and **creolization** are natural communicative and linguistic processes, which are not restricted to the modern period. The pidgin Sabir, for example, developed as early as the crusades and became widely used within and outside the Mediterranean world. Since most pidgins (and creoles) show surprising structural similarities, their origin is a highly controversial issue: theories of origin range from the claim that all pidgins go back to a single source, possibly Sabir, which underwent multiple **relexification**, i.e. exchange of vocabulary, through lexical borrowing, to the view that they have arisen independently in similar communicative contexts, possibly as the result of an inbuilt universal 'bioprogram' for language acquisition which all humans share.

In the development of a pidgin, there is contact between speakers of a dominant language with those of one or more subordinate, so-called substrate, languages. The status of the speakers corresponds to that of their languages, with substrate language speakers typically being native labourers and slaves. It has been argued that the simple grammatical structure of pidgins is derived from the subordinate language(s), though this seems unlikely given the astonishing structural similarities among pidgins in different parts of the world. What is more certain, and generally accepted, is that the restricted vocabulary of pidgins is mainly derived from the dominant language, often one of the main colonial languages such as English or French, a fact which has contributed to the mistaken belief that pidgins (and creoles) are corrupt forms of these languages. Pidgins with English-based vocabulary include West African Pidgin English, and Tok Pisin in Papua New Guinea; Haitian Creole is French-based, Senegal Creole is Portuguese-based, etc. Typical linguistic features of pidgins are: strong variation in pronunciation, combined with a reduced phonological system, i.e. fewer vowels and consonants than in the dominant language, so that there is, for example, no phonological distinction between *sip*, *ship*, *chip* in Tok Pisin; simplification of morphology and syntax, especially lack of inflections indicating number, case, person, and gender, lack of tense markers to indicate time, fixed word order, lack of sentence embedding, i.e. of clausal subordination, etc.; finally, a restricted vocabulary, which may be expanded in an ad hoc manner from native languages.

In the process of creolization, these simple structures get elaborated in a variety of ways: morphology and syntax become more complex, the vocabulary increases, and pronunciation becomes more stable—processes which are mainly due to the above-mentioned additional functions of a first language. A well-documented case is Tok Pisin, which has become the first language of a considerable number of speakers and at the same time one of the national and parliamentary languages of Papua New Guinea, where it serves as a **lingua franca**, a general language of communication, for many more people. As a first language, Tok Pisin is generally spoken faster and has thus undergone phonological processes of assimilation and reduction (e.g. the demonstrative/article *wanpela* (< *one fellow*) has been reduced to *-la*). It has acquired new grammatical categories such as number and tense, partly through grammaticalization, such as *bin* for marking past time and *bə/bai* as a verbal prefix for marking future time (< *baimbai*, originally a sentence adverb meaning 'later'; cf. English *by and by*) (see also Readings, Text 15); it has developed more complex sentence structures with embedded relative clauses. New compounds as well as prefixed and suffixed words testify to productive word-formation rules (*skinwara* 'sweat' replacing the older *wara bilong skin* 'water of skin'), though there is also extensive borrowing from English. It has even developed different varieties and some stylistic differentiation. From a typological point of view it is noteworthy that in creolization free grammatical markers may develop into bound morphemes through phonological reduction (cf. above for *bɘbai*), so that certain isolating structures change into agglutinating ones (cf. Chapter 4).

Most of the structural changes in Tok Pisin have happened within one or two generations and have thus been directly observable. This has forced historical linguists to reconsider some of the traditional views about the nature and rate of linguistic change, though there is some disagreement whether changes in creoles can really be compared with those in other languages.

However, on purely linguistic grounds, the distinction between pidgins, creoles, and other languages is not always as clear-cut as the above discussion might imply. If a creole coexists with its originally dominant language in the same area for some time, such as Jamaican Creole English and Standard English in Jamaica, a process of **decreolization** may begin, where speakers increasingly replace the creole structures with those of the dominant language. This may result in a linguistic continuum from the creole through various intermediate varieties to the respective standard language—though all these varieties may be used by the same speaker in different situations. Decreolization may eventually lead to the disappearance or 'death' of the creole and there are claims that African-American Vernacular English (AAVE) is the result of decreolization. There are also, however, other types of language death which are closely connected with linguistic change.

Language death

Languages which are no longer spoken, like Latin, are often referred to as dead languages. But this is misleading. For Latin is not 'dead' in the same way as, for example, Cornish or

Tasmanian are. These are extinct, whereas Latin still survives. Not only does it occur in certain ritual uses in religious and academic life, but it has survived in transmuted form as it gradually developed into the Romance languages French, Italian, Spanish, etc., as we saw in Chapter 2. In a similar way, Ancient Greek (another language sometimes referred to as dead) developed into Modern Greek, or Old English into Modern English. Indeed from a purely linguistic point of view it is difficult to decide when Latin (or rather its spoken form Vulgar Latin) 'became' Old French or Old Spanish, and extralinguistic events may be more important for such a dating than purely linguistic ones.

The term 'language death' does not apply to such cases as these but rather to the extinction of a language, its complete disappearance without trace, or with traces only in recorded form. This may happen in two ways. In the first case, a language dies because its speakers do, for reasons of disease, natural disaster, or genocide. An infamous example is the fate of Tasmanian, whose speakers were first infected by disease brought unwittingly by the Europeans, and then deliberately slaughtered by British troops. Similar fates at the hands of European settlers destroyed many Amerindian and Australian indigenous speech communities. In these cases, fully developed and still fully vigorous languages disappeared, often without a trace, because their speakers were killed off. This first kind of language death is the result of a (calamitous) contact between communities and not their languages, and has nothing to do with linguistics as such.

The second kind of language death does bring linguistic issues to the fore, and is the result of intensive language contact. This occurs when the people survive but their language does not. Speakers give up their language gradually and knowingly (and even to a degree voluntarily) as its functions are taken over by a more powerful rival. This typically occurs after an extended period of bilingualism, during which there is a reduction of the social functions, and in consequence the grammatical and lexical complexity, of the dying language.

A variety of social, political, and economic factors may cause this process, in which the speech community shifts from the less prestigious language to the more prestigious and powerful one, as with the Celtic languages Cornish and Manx in Britain. More rarely, the dominating group abandons their language in favour of the originally less prestigious language, either for demographic or political reasons. This happened with the Germanic language of the Franks in medieval France and with Anglo-French in medieval Britain. Today many languages are endangered, not least because of the widespread dominance of English (e.g. Irish, Welsh, Hawaiian, Maori, Australian aboriginal languages).

When speakers shift to another language, their own language becomes more and more restricted in its range of use and, as a result, its grammatical and lexical resources begin to atrophy by inaction. At the same time, of course, this impoverishes the input necessary for the acquisition process, since children learning a dying language are exposed only to sparse data to learn from. As a consequence, we find reduction of grammatical structures, such as the replacement of suffixes by free forms and the disappearance of inflections, which may lead to fixed word order. There is also borrowing of grammatical structures from the dominant language as well as increasing replacement of native vocabulary by borrowings. In addition, children will no longer be exposed to the more intricate features of the language which encode nuances of social meaning. Since it is these which typically give a language its unique identity, children will have increasingly less in the way of linguistic distinctiveness to identify with. In such situations, within a generation or two, speakers become 'semi-speakers' in the sense that though they may retain extensive passive (i.e. receptive) competence in the language, their productive competence becomes gradually reduced and they consequently have less and less to pass on to their children. These changes have been observed among Breton speakers in France, among Hungarian speakers in Austria, and in numerous other bilingual speech communities. In the end the language may gradually die out by the law of diminishing returns. Many or most of these changes also occur in normal language change, as the development of English after the Norman Conquest of 1066 testifies, but they happen at an unusually high speed in a dying language. Language death itself, though, may be a rather slow process.

However, even in death there is some life, in that some grammatical or lexical features of the abandoned language may survive as a **substratum** in the new language and give it a distinctive character (see also Readings, Text 14). These substrate features, traces of the old language, can serve as markers of ethnic or national identity long after the original language itself has disappeared, as is the case, for example, with particular features of pronunciation, grammar, and vocabulary in Irish and Scottish English, which go back to Gaelic.

Language birth and language death offer linguists unique opportunities for observing rather rapid linguistic changes in extreme forms of language contact. But there are also ways of observing the more gradual changes happening in ordinary languages, as will become apparent in the next chapter.

7

How and why do languages change?

One obvious answer to the question why languages change in general is that everything changes in human affairs. It would be surprising if languages did *not* change. The interesting question is why particular changes take place. Why do vowels shift in a specific way, why do grammatical or lexical features of a language change or disappear at a particular time?

Such questions have occupied linguists for a long time and an amazing number of 'explanations' have been proposed, some of them also by non-specialists. It has been suggested that change is brought about under the influence of geography or climate, so that mountains, snowy tundra, or rainforest will leave their inevitable mark on the languages spoken there. It has also been suggested that it is not external geography but internal anatomy which determines the form of changes, that the speech organs of human beings of certain ethnic origin are somehow less pliable than others, and so leave their mark on pronunciation. Another explanation is that languages change simply because people are too lazy to speak them 'properly', implying that if they were more careful about their language it would not change at all.

Historical linguistics has more reasonable, and acceptable explanations to offer, although these are not the ones characteristic of the natural sciences. The latter provide strictly causal and universally valid laws which also allow for predictions, while the explanations of linguistics are of a probabilistic kind. Three general types of explanation of linguistic change deserve our consideration, namely (i) *functional explanations*, which focus on language as an abstract system in which system-internal forces operate and lead to change; (ii) *psycholinguistic explanations*, which concentrate on the cognitive and psycholinguistic processes inside the speaker's head; (iii) *sociolinguistic explanations*, which see the reasons for change in the roles of speakers as social beings.

Functional explanations

In functional thinking, linguistic systems are seen as having a natural tendency to regulate themselves, and linguistic change as basically therapeutic in that it makes systems more symmetrical and balanced, and therefore simpler.

Let us begin with an example of a therapeutic change from the history of English. Before the eighteenth century, English had eight fricative phonemes; six of these were arranged in pairs distinguished by the phonological feature [voiced], i.e. by the presence or absence of voicing, namely /f/–/v/; /θ/–/ð/; /s/–/z/. The remaining two voiceless phonemes /ʃ/ and /h/, however, had no voiced partner, so that the subsystem of fricatives was obviously asymmetrical. From the eighteenth century on, English began to develop /ʒ/, the voiced partner for /ʃ/, both through the borrowing of French loan words (*beige*, *rouge*) and through the sound change from /zj/ > /ʒ/ in words like *pleasure*, *treasure*. Though this change is partly due to structural borrowing from French, it can be interpreted as therapeutic in that it had the beneficial effect of establishing symmetry in this subsystem. The second asymmetrical phoneme, /h/, on the other hand, has disappeared from a number of vernacular varieties of British English by 'h-dropping', thus restoring the symmetry by eliminating the 'odd man out'. This striving for symmetry and balance is at the same time a move towards greater economy of linguistic systems.

Phonological processes such as chain shifts with their push or drag chain mechanisms (cf. Chapter 5) have also been claimed to serve various therapeutic functions. Among these are the tendency to avoid phonemic merger, to keep or restore the balance of the phonemic system, or to increase the phonetic space between phonemes. This in turn may also have the effect of avoiding homonyms, i.e. two words of identical form but different meaning. However, in cases where two homonymic words with conflicting meanings have developed, a therapeutic change can also be brought about by the disappearance of one of these words to avoid 'homonymic clash' (see the example of English *let* discussed in Chapter 3).

A basic problem with such functional explanations is how the individual speakers or the speech community as a whole could know about the actual or threatening asymmetry of systems and act accordingly. Another problem with the notion of 'therapeutic change' is that therapeutic changes in one part of the grammar may create imbalance in another part; finally, if this was the main driving force behind change then we would expect all linguistic systems to have become balanced by now, which they clearly are not.

Another functional concept for explaining change is that of **functional load**, i.e. the number of functions a particular linguistic item has. Thus the phonemic opposition between /t/ and /d/ has a high functional load since it establishes a large number of minimal pairs, i.e. word pairs which only differ in a single phoneme, such as *tip–dip*, *trip–drip*, *sat–sad*, etc. It has been claimed that such items are more resistant to change than those with a low functional load such as that between /n/ and the velar nasal /ŋ/ in *sin* and *sing*, whose merger would cause less communicative damage.

The functional load of specific phonological features seems to be even more relevant for phonological change than that of individual phonemes. The distinctive feature [voiced], for example, is central in the structuring of the English consonantal system, and accordingly it has an extremely high functional load; compare the oppositions between voiceless /p, t, k, f, ʃ/ and voiced /b, d, g, v, ʒ/, which establish numerous minimal pairs such as *pit–bit*, *tip–dip*, *cold–gold*, etc., and have therefore high communicative relevance. This feature also establishes less central phonemic oppositions with low functional load such as English /θ/ vs. /ð/, or /s/ vs. /z/, as in *thigh–thy, seal–zeal*. Here the high functional load of the phonological feature [voiced] in the overall system provides an explanation for the surprising stability of these peripheral phonemic pairs.

However, though linguistic factors such as functional load undoubtedly *can* contribute to linguistic change, there is no empirical proof of their coming into play in specific cases.

Psycholinguistic explanations: language acquisition

Psycholinguistic explanations of change focus on the cognitive processes in the brain of the speaker and are particularly related to the different versions of generative theories of language as first developed by Noam Chomsky. These theories, which have developed highly formalized models of grammar, see human beings as being endowed with an innate faculty for acquiring language, which has been variously conceived as a Language Acquisition Device (LAD), a Universal Grammar (UG), a bio-program, or a number of pre-set parameters (i.e. human beings are seen as 'being wired for language'). In the process of language acquisition, children activate this faculty for constructing the rules for their mental grammar by building hypotheses based on the input of utterances they hear from competent, especially adult speakers. Since this hypothesis building is not always done perfectly, differences to the grammar of the adult speakers may arise. Language acquisition by children is thus regarded as the prime factor in language change by psycholinguistic theories, and most types of change have been claimed to be restricted to language acquisition. This implies that most changes in the speakers' grammar take place between different generations of speakers. In earlier versions of such theories, linguistic, especially phonological, change was seen as due to changes in the formalized productive rules of grammar, such as rule addition, loss, or reordering of rules (see also Readings, Text 11).

In recent years, generative theories have increasingly focused on syntactic change, and detailed proposals for the mechanisms of such change have been made. These rely heavily on the concept of the 'restructuring' of grammars, a special type of grammatical reanalysis of the whole grammatical system or a subsystem. As stated above, the hypotheses which children form about the structure of grammar are based on the input of utterances they hear. Though children tend to construct optimal grammars by means of their innate faculty, their hypotheses may deviate from the grammar of the adult speakers in certain minor aspects. In the course of time, however, such minor deviations accumulate until the grammar may finally become too complex to be easily learnable by the child. At this point an abrupt and fundamental restructuring may occur, which results in a different analysis and thus in a change of the underlying grammar. An essential aspect of this view is that syntactic change is autonomous, i.e. it occurs independently from other linguistic and extralinguistic factors.

In spite of the obvious attractions of this explanation, many of its general axioms have been severely criticized on theoretical grounds, and some of the explanations of specific changes, such as the development of English modals from full verbs, have been shown not to be substantiated by textual evidence. Furthermore, we have conclusive empirical evidence that linguistic change in general, and syntactic change in particular, is not restricted to language acquisition, but may also occur with adult speakers.

Sociolinguistic explanations

The language change that we have been discussing in the previous chapters is, of course, a continuous process and is as evident in the present as in the past. Yet it is only in relatively recent times that linguists have plotted change as it is actually happening. Previously, the received linguistic wisdom was that language change could never be directly observed (apart from the obvious adoption of new words) but had to be inferred indirectly by reference to older stages of the language concerned. In fact, the consideration of change was not included in the agenda of most twentieth-century models of linguistic description up to the end of the 1960s. These were mainly based on an idealization of data which represented language as a static system of formal rules and relations, focusing particularly on phonology and the syntactic properties of sentences. Such idealization was a methodological convenience which enabled linguists to avoid the distracting details of how language actually operates in order to identify certain essential and apparently stable features of language. Whatever may have been achieved by this idealization, it is clear that such an assumption could not, of its nature, take account of language as a continuous process.

There are two major indicators of change in particular which idealized formalist models cannot deal with. Since they represent language as a well defined system with clear-cut categories, they cannot, obviously, deal with phenomena which are *not* clear-cut.

They cannot cope with fuzziness. And since they represent this system as homogeneous, in a state of steady uniformity, they cannot, equally obviously, deal with variation. Both of these, however, are crucial to an understanding of the actual process of language change.

Fuzziness. Formalist linguistics seeks to describe language in terms of well defined categories. A noun is a noun, a verb is a verb, a sentence is either grammatically well formed or it is not. But when we look at language in use, things are not so straightforward. Most of us are aware that we repeatedly hear and produce utterances which seem to be not quite correct, though not really wrong either. A case in point is the use of the English progressive form with verbs expressing a state, as in *Mary is knowing the answer*. This for some speakers is ungrammatical, while others may not be so sure about it. In other words, there is evidently a fuzzy area in which judgements about grammaticality are not as clear-cut as grammarians would like them to be. Such fuzziness may be an important indicator of ongoing changes, because in such cases speakers evidently no longer stick to established rules or norms, but begin to extend the validity of a rule to new environments. But one problem with fuzziness is that it is elusive, difficult to pin down in any systematic way.

Variation. With variation, the second indicator of change, we are on more secure empirical ground. Linguists have, of course, been aware of variation for a long time. If they excluded it from their accounts this was because it was inconvenient for their particular kind of enquiry, not because they did not know about it. They simply assumed that it was a more or less random and trivial phenomenon, which could not be accounted for in any systematic way. It was the American linguist William Labov who realized that the careful analysis of linguistic variation combined with sociologically oriented statistics might tell us a lot about the relation between the synchronic state and the diachronic development of a language.

Though Labov's main interest was in the social dimension of linguistic change in contemporary American English, he was equally interested in the general properties of linguistic change as such. Labov adopted the so-called uniformitarian principle: general principles of change in former times are not fundamentally different in kind from those governing changes happening at the present time. Moreover, he realized that language change over time is closely related to language variation at any one moment in time, and that we could use insights from contemporary sociolinguistic studies about language variation in the present to explain the phenomenon of language change in the past.

This is how the principle works. In every language most, if not all, speakers have a varied linguistic repertoire in the sense that they have more than one 'version' or **variant** of many linguistic items at their disposal, which they tend to use at different times. Some of these different variants appear to have particular social significance for the speech community concerned. Examples of such **linguistic variables** are the (r) variable in New York City, i.e. the presence or absence of post-vocalic [r] in words like *car*, *cart*, the (ing) variable in varieties of British English, i.e. the pronunciation of the suffix *-ing* as in *going* as either [ɪŋ] or [ɪn], but also different vowel qualities such as the variable (a) in Belfast, i.e. different realisations of /æ/ before various consonants.

The fluctuating realization of such variables can be associated with certain groups of speakers, so that people of a certain age or sex, ethnic group or social class will 'typically' use a particular variant: one group tends to use more *r*s than another one in the *car*/*cart* set of words, and so on. Depending on the group, certain variants will be stigmatized as marking inferiority of some kind. But although one might identify certain groups as typically using a particular variant, they may not use it all the time. And here things get interesting. It turns out that if people are asked to produce speech under certain circumstances, they will tend to produce one variant more frequently at one time and a different one at another. More precisely, two decisive parameters which influence speakers' linguistic behaviour are their social class membership and the formality of the situation. In a famous study of New York speech, Labov selected a range of speakers from different social groups and elicited their speech by giving them lists of words and texts to read aloud, and engaging them in both formal interviews and informal conversations. What emerged was that *r* was inserted more frequently in the speech of the upper middle class than in that of the lower middle and working classes. Furthermore, all speakers changed the frequency of variants according to the kind of activity they were involved in. The more formal the situation, i.e. the more attention people paid to their actual speech, the more frequently they pronounced the *r*; conversely, the sound tended to be much less used in informal situations, especially when people were emotionally involved in what they were saying. This pattern emerged with *all* social classes, even though the lower the social class the fewer *r*s were produced in all situations. This is a clear indication that *r*-pronunciation has social prestige. But there is one significant exception to this general pattern: the lower-middle-class speakers actually produced *more r*s in the formal speech situations than those in the social class above them. This surprising linguistic behaviour can be explained as a result of the linguistic and social insecurity of lower-middle-class speakers, and their desire to identify with the more prestigious group above them. When they pay more attention to their speech, they overuse what they take to be the prestige variant. This is a phenomenon Labov refers to as **hypercorrection**.

This finding is of considerable significance because it can be interpreted as an indication of a change in progress. However, this assumption has to be substantiated by further evidence. Other available data show that New York speech in general was practically *r*-less in the thirties, as is evident, for example, in films of that period. We may thus conclude that the pattern of variation that occurs at one time reflects a general trend over time, the increased use of [r] being motivated by the desire for upward mobility to higher social class membership.

However, with regard to the direction of change, Labov observed two different types: first, changes which move towards the established norms and are brought about consciously, labelled 'changes from above'; second, the unconscious 'changes from below', which lead away from standard linguistic norms. Changes from above seem to be mainly carried by women, for whom the *overt* prestige of linguistic standards is more important; changes from below, on the other hand, are predominantly carried by men, for whom the *covert* prestige of non-standard varieties, connected with working-class values of toughness, crude language, and group solidarity, are more important (see also Readings, Text 18).

In the case just considered, the crucial factor affecting variation is social class. Another factor is age. The differences in the way different age groups realize a linguistic variable at a particular time can also provide us with clear pointers to language change in progress. The same assumptions are made as with social class differences. That is to say, it is assumed that we can infer how a language will develop over time from the analysis of a variable situation between different age groups at one point in time (the so-called **apparent-time analysis**). Thus a consistently higher frequency of a particular variant among younger speakers will be read as evidence of a change in progress whereby this variant will gradually replace the one predominantly used by older speakers.

But we need to be circumspect about such conclusions from apparent-time analyses of this kind. For example, it is a well attested fact that particularly young speakers use specific linguistic features as identity markers, but give them up in later life. That is, instead of keeping their way of speaking as they grow older, thereby slowly replacing the variants used by the speakers of the previous generations, they themselves grow out of their earlier way of speaking. Charting change by relating current variation to situations in the past, as when tracing the fortunes of the (r) variable, is relatively uncontroversial. But projecting the future from the present is a different matter. While an apparent-time analysis shows patterns of distribution and use of linguistic forms which *may* indicate a spreading change, it should be complemented by a **real-time analysis**, i.e. an analysis of the same speech community at different points in time. It is this complementary use of apparent-time and real-time analyses that characterizes the most significant current work in language variation and change, work which has deeply affected our understanding of how linguistic change works.

Labov's discovery that variation is the basis of every linguistic change (even though not every variation may lead to change) was a major breakthrough in linguistics. Though variation is an inherent property of language, it originates from a range of extralinguistic and linguistic factors, such as language contact, phonetic and structural or functional factors. Furthermore, different variants may coexist over a considerable period of time.

Only with the social marking of a specific variant and its socially conditioned spread through the speech community does language change take place. The discovery of the close interdependence of variation and change has also led to the abandoning of the strict separation between synchronic and diachronic linguistics.

It should be noted that the sociolinguistic approach outlined here does not completely dismiss functional aspects, but rather integrates them as secondary and subordinate factors.

Labov's approach to language change is basically 'macro-sociolinguistic' and looks at society as a whole. An alternative is to take a 'micro-sociolinguistic' view by looking at the more specific social networks in which speakers live and communicate. The nature and density of such networks may differ considerably, as does the intensity of contacts with speakers from other networks. Research carried out by L. and J. Milroy in Belfast working-class speech communities has shown that linguistic change may depend on factors such as structure and density of networks, the speakers' status within their own network and the degree of contact with speakers outside their central network.

The origin and spread of changes

The work we have been considering raises a number of problematic issues concerning the explanation of language change. One of these has to do with the nature of **constraints** determining which linguistic changes are possible and which are not. There is evidently no list of universally valid restrictions, which would enable predictions to be made about which changes will happen in what circumstances. However, we have already come across various proposals for constraints on changes in previous chapters: among these were the implicational universals of basic word order types such as SVO, SOV, etc., or the view that certain morphological and phonological changes are more 'natural' than others. All these, however, seem to be general tendencies or probabilities of occurrence rather than strict rules (if we disregard constraints on sound change resulting from the form and movements of the speech organs).

Apart from such linguistic constraints, social or solidarity constraints have been proposed as forces preventing specific changes from occurring, such as the change towards a standard pronunciation in a close-knit non-standard speech community; but such social constraints are even more context-dependent than linguistic ones.

A second issue concerns the factors that trigger off or actuate change in the first place. It is puzzling that a particular change happens in a particular language at a specific point in time but not at another time or in another language in the same linguistic context. A rather promising though still not fully accepted social explanation for the **actuation** of change has been proposed for close-knit Belfast working-class communities within the Milroys' social-network model mentioned above. These working-class networks are characterized by a particular set of shared values and have a specific internal structure. There are core members with rather few outside contacts and more peripheral members who interact more frequently with speakers from outside their community. These peripheral members regularly show innovations in their speech as a result of their multiple linguistic and social contacts. Such so-called 'speaker-innovations' are generally not adopted by the group as a whole, whose conservative core members stick to their in-group linguistic norms. Only under specific circumstances, such as when a larger number of peripheral members show the same speaker-innovations, may the core members begin to adopt an innovation, thus leading to language change. This basic distinction between the innovations adopted by an individual, and language change as adoption of a new feature by the group or speech community as a whole, would account for the fact that changes take place at certain specific times, and not at others. However, it remains to be seen whether this model also works for other social groups or in different cultures, and what other factors might be found in the future to explain how change is initiated. (See also Readings, Text 16.)

A third issue concerns the **implementation** of change: how changes spread in the linguistic system of both individual speakers and specific speech communities. This issue is best illustrated by reference to phonological change.

There are two general views on the implementation of phonological change, both still highly controversial. The first characterizes it as phonetically gradual, and lexically abrupt, claiming that sound change operates by imperceptible small phonetic changes but affects simultaneously all words in which the respective sound occurs in identical phonetic environments. This is the so-called Neogrammarian hypothesis (after the German Neogrammarian linguistic school of the late nineteenth century), which was the dominant position up to the 1960s. Let us take a closer look at this view. The first part of the claim, that of phonetic gradualness, may seem plausible for changes of vowel quality such as [o:] > [u:], [e:] > [i:], or possibly of vowel quantity, but there are evidently also changes that cannot be phonetically gradual. Neither the insertion or deletion of sounds nor their rearrangement ('metathesis') as in Old English *acsian* beside *ascian* 'ask', can happen gradually, and the same applies to the change from a stop [p] to a fricative [f], or to devoicing, i.e. the loss of the feature [voiced], etc. In other words, some changes may be phonetically gradual, while others are clearly phonetically abrupt.

Now to the second part of this view: does a change affect all possible words at the same time, as the **regularity hypothesis** of the Neogrammarians would have it, claiming that sound change was regular and without exceptions, like the 'laws of nature'? This position has been challenged in what is known as the theory of **lexical diffusion**. There is evidence that phonological change is lexically gradual, i.e. that it affects only part of the possible words or morphemes at a given time, and spreads gradually through the vocabulary of a language. This diffusion of change through the vocabulary is not linear, but shows a 'slow-quick-slow' pattern. In the initial stage, only a small percentage of the eligible words are affected, followed by a shorter period of rapid change, in which a major part adopts the change; in the final stage the change slows down again and affects the remaining forms. Frequently some unchanged relic forms remain, which thus appear as irregularities or 'exceptions' from a synchronic point of view. Such exceptions to otherwise regular changes have been a problem for the regularity hypothesis and were sometimes explained as the result of dialect contact or dialect mixing.

An interesting example of diffusion of change in English is 'yod-dropping', i.e. the deletion of [j] in words like *tune*, etc. It began as early as the seventeenth century and is still going on today, with clear differences between various regional and national varieties of English. The spread of this change is phonetically conditioned and depends on the nature of the preceding consonant. There seems to be a generally valid pattern of yod-deletion and -retention, which has been formalized into the following 'implicational scale' by L. Bauer:

s > θ > l > n, d, t

This scale predicts that a speaker pronouncing [j] after [s] will also retain it after any of the consonants to the right of [s], i.e. speakers saying [sjuːtɪd] *suited* will also pronounce [j] in *enthusiasm* or *tune*; on the other hand, people pronouncing [ljuːsɪd] *lucid* will also keep the [j] in *tutor*, but not necessarily in *suited*. In other words, if [j] is retained after a consonant at any point on the scale, this implies the retention of [j] after all consonants to the right of that point, but does not say anything about its retention to the left of that consonant. Similar implicational patterns of change have already been discussed in Chapter 4 in the case of syntactic typologies and changes in the basic word order.

In spite of such evidence, lexical diffusion has not been generally accepted as a model for the spread of phonological change in historical linguistics (see also Readings, Text 17). Recent research makes it seem likely that both types of spread may exist side by side in a language, with certain sound changes being of the Neogrammarian type, and others following the pattern of lexical diffusion.

The above discussion has concentrated on the implementation of change in the linguistic system without regard to the social dimension of the implementation in the speech community. In Labov's macro-sociolinguistic model, the decisive step is that various social factors may cause an existing variant to become socially significant for the group identification of speakers. This entails that this variant also becomes grammatically significant, since the rules for its fluctuating use, the so-called 'variable rules', become an integral part of a speaker's competence. In other words, a member of a specific social group somehow knows the probability of occurrence of a variant, and knows which variant to use in a given speech style with what overall frequency, as was illustrated at the beginning of this chapter. Gradually, such variable rules may be extended to new linguistic environments as well as to new groups of speakers with whom the first group interacts. In the course of this process, the original social marking of a variant may change, e.g. from 'vulgar' to 'informal' or 'progressive'. A case in point is the originally non-standard London Cockney feature of the 'glottal stop' instead of the alveolar stop [t] in words like *butter*, *what*, which has entered some progressive forms of standard English, especially in final position.

If a specific variant has become more or less accepted by the whole speech community, it becomes unmarked and the original variable rule evidently ceases to operate. In Labov's view this pattern of spread has been observed in all contemporary sound changes and should also be accepted as the pattern of implementation of earlier changes.

However, changes over a large geographical area do not always spread gradually from one area to a neighbouring one, but often jump from one large urban centre to another, leaving the area in between unaffected, at least for a time.

The present chapter has shown that, in spite of the long tradition of historical linguistics and recent intensive research, there is still no generally accepted answer to the question of how and why languages change, though many important insights have been gained in the last decades. The above survey has sketched the three main theoretical approaches to the problem, but it is in no way complete and had to neglect a number of less mainstream, though still interesting proposals (see also Readings, Text 19). Discussions in the specialist literature are often extremely controversial, and the explanations of one school of linguistics tend to be utterly condemned by another one. Much of the controversy is linked to what we understand by explanation, and how we view language—as an autonomous system, as a psychological or biological fact, or as a vehicle of communication which speakers use. Language is certainly all that and much more, but one thing should be absolutely clear: languages which have no speakers do not change—and thus any explanation which does not also somehow consider the speaker can never fully explain language change.

8

Postscript: further developments

As has been stressed throughout this book, historical linguistics is itself subject to history, and the study of language change itself changes with the times. Among the new developments, the following three have become particularly prominent or promising over recent years. First, a focus on the social and pragmatic factors of language use in the study of older language states; second, work on linguistic evolution within a neo-Darwinian framework; and third, the deliberate instigation of change in language planning.

Socio-historical linguistics and historical pragmatics

Advances in the sociolinguistic study of current changes as well as in pragmatics, i.e. the study of language in context, have led to an increased awareness of the importance of speaker-related factors for the study of older language stages. This has been accompanied by the methodological developments brought about by advances in computer technology, which provides vastly improved facilities for the accumulation and analysis of data.

The sociolinguistic approach discussed in Chapter 7 focuses on variation in modern spoken language as an indication of ongoing changes. According to the uniformitarian principle, the insights thus gained from the present can be applied to explain the linguistic changes in the past. *Socio-historical linguistics* tries to discover the social factors of language change in earlier periods by analysing large computer-readable text corpora containing a carefully balanced selection of older texts. These texts are chosen according to independent variables such as the sex and age of the author, the purpose and audience of the text, text type and genre, the level of formality, the closeness to spoken language, etc. These social and textual variables are systematically correlated with the extensive linguistic variation found in older texts. The different and changing frequencies of specific linguistic variants in relation to the different social and textual variables, and in relation to time, can serve as indicators of change in a similar way to the variation in the modern speech. Socio-historical linguistics has to work in an interdisciplinary way, integrating historical, demographic, and sociological information on the periods investigated.

In a similar way, *historical pragmatics* investigates language not as an abstract system, but concentrates on what speakers actually do with language in interaction in a specific context. A growing number of studies investigate older stages of languages and their diachronic developments from such a pragmatic point of view, even though there is still no full agreement on the scope and methodology of the new discipline. Especially interactional and dialogic texts such as letters, drama, political debates or transcriptions of court records, which are increasingly available in English and other European languages from at least the fifteenth century onwards, provide valuable data for pragmatic analysis. The study of forms of address, such as Early Modern English *you* vs. *thou*, already has some tradition, but has received renewed attention in sociolinguistic and pragmatic frameworks, which provide concepts such as power and solidarity. Further important topics are 'speech acts' such as 'apologizing', 'requesting', and 'verbal duelling', which relate to more general questions of and changes in linguistic politeness in a specific, historically determined culture. Further research issues are the development of pragmatically relevant linguistic elements, such as discourse markers, i.e. elements which have specific functions in discourse and structure it in specific ways.

Evolutionary linguistics

Historical linguistics has always drawn profitably on insights from other disciplines. As early as the nineteenth century, the uniformitarian principle was adopted from geology, and biology provided the idea of the family tree model of genetic linguistic relationships. In recent times sociology and statistics have made valuable contributions to the field. One of the most recent influences comes from biology, more precisely from insights from neo-Darwinian evolutionary theory. In early nineteenth-century pre-Darwinian thinking, linguistic evolution had been seen as a progression from a more primitive to an ideal state of language, followed by a period of decay and finally of death. Darwinian evolution, however, does not see evolution as either progress or decay, but as a basically neutral process of random mutation leading to variation, with natural selection from among the existing variants leading to change. This bears obvious similarities with the way in which the interaction between variation and language change is viewed today (see Chapter 7). More recently, concepts from modern biology, such as the role of genes in biological replication or copying, as well as Dawkins's 'memes' have been integrated into different new models of linguistic change, though such theories are still controversial. (For further details, see Readings, Text 20.)

As we have said before, historical linguistics has to be seen in the context of its time, and this recent biological orientation of historical linguistics may reflect to some extent the shift from the long dominance of sociology to that of biology both in science and in our daily lives.

Standardization and language planning

The majority of linguistic changes discussed so far happen 'naturally' and unintentionally. However, language is sometimes also consciously changed, by official institutions or influential pressure groups, either as a result of political centralization, or, more recently, through the influence of the media, capitalist economics, and moves towards political correctness.

One widespread type of linguistic intervention is *standardization*, i.e. the choice of a variety as a nationally accepted medium of communication. Standard languages are widely codified in grammars and dictionaries and thus easily teachable. In general, standardization reduces the natural linguistic variation by decreeing one variant as 'correct' and stigmatizing other variants as incorrect and non-standard. In many parts of the world standardization has been going on for centuries, carried out either by official 'language academies' or, as in the case of Britain, by prestigious individuals (see Chapter 1).

Standardization is a special, possibly the most important, type of **language planning**. In the twentieth century, language planning by governmental institutions has become particularly important in many former colonies which tried to establish indigenous languages as national standards. When Indonesia became independent after the Second World War, Bahasa Indonesia was chosen as the new national language in place of Dutch. Since it had formerly been restricted to 'lower' functions in the private domains, it lacked technical and abstract vocabulary for a range of new 'higher' functions in the public domains. An official committee was appointed to develop the necessary terminology, by coining new complex words, by extending the meanings of existing words, but only rarely by borrowing. The acceptance of such measures depends to a large extent on the ability and willingness of the educational system as well as the media to spread these innovations, and above all on the positive attitude of speakers towards this process. In the case of Bahasa Indonesia, and similarly of Hebrew, these measures have succeeded, while in other cases, such as Irish, governmental intervention has not found sufficient public support. (See also Readings, Text 21.)

Another area of conscious intervention involves attempts to eliminate sexist and racist language. These have been quite successful in printed English, where the media, publishing companies, and official institutions have issued guidelines on politically correct language. Compounds with *man* such as *chairman* or *mankind* are increasingly being replaced by the neutral terms *chair(person)* and *humankind* when referring to people of both sexes. Lack of syntactic concord as in 'Everybody took their books', though still criticized by purists, has become widely accepted to avoid the sexist 'his book' or the clumsy 'his or her books'. There is still no generally accepted solution for the avoidance of the use of *he* to refer to both sexes ('generic *he*'), but generic *she* is increasingly used by female writers. In the same way racially, ethnically, or religiously loaded terms have been widely banned from written language, though they are still often used in speech. As with standardization, such issues seem to be only successful if they find wide acceptance in society and are promoted by the educational system and the media.

Conclusion

The previous chapters have tried to survey the wide scope and changing emphases of historical linguistics, though the presentation was necessarily selective and incomplete. As the linguistic discipline with the longest research tradition, historical linguistics has seen numerous shifts of theoretical perspective as well as shifts in general scholarly acceptance. It has both widely influenced other disciplines and been open to new impulses from outside. Language is the most human property we have and, together with other historical disciplines, the study of language change can fundamentally contribute to our understanding of our past history as well as of our present condition as human beings endowed with language. Humans have adapted in a multitude of ways to the changing environment and the changing social conditions which they create and in which they exist, and language has been part of this adaptive human behaviour and our changing social identities. For this reason the study of the history of language may help us to understand better some of the fundamental issues of humanity.

Readings

Chapter 1
Language change as a matter of fact

Text 1

JAMES MILROY *and* LESLEY MILROY: *Authority in Language: Investigating Standard English* (3rd edn.). Routledge 1999, pages 30–1

Objections to language change often appeal to the need to preserve the standard language. This text discusses how a 'complaint tradition' has served this role in the preservation of Standard English.

The norms of written and formal English have ... been codified in dictionaries, grammars and handbooks of usage and inculcated by prescription through the educational system. ... Outside the schoolroom, the standard ideology has been most openly promoted by writers in what we have called 'the complaint tradition'. This tradition can, however, be divided into two broad types. ...

Type 1 complaints, which are implicitly legalistic and which are concerned with correctness, attack 'mis-use' of specific parts of the phonology, grammar, vocabulary of English ... Type 2 complaints, which we may call 'moralistic', recommend clarity in writing and attack what appear to be abuses of language that may mislead and confuse the public. ... The correctness tradition (Type 1) is wholly dedicated to the maintenance of the norms of Standard English in preference to other varieties: sometimes writers in this tradition attempt to justify the usages they favour and condemn those they dislike by appeals to logic, etymology and so forth. Very often, however, they make no attempt what-ever to explain why one usage is correct and another incorrect: they simply take it for granted that the proscribed form is *obviously* unacceptable and illegitimate; in short, they believe in a transcendental norm of correct English.

▷ *Do you think these observations are also valid for standard languages other than English?*

▷ *What is the relationship between complaints about correctness (Type 1 above) and attitudes to language change?*

▷ *Do you think that speakers of non-standardized languages might also complain about linguistic 'decay' and 'corruption'? If so, why?*

Chapter 2

Reconstructing the past: data and evidence

Text 2

ANTHONY FOX: *Linguistic Reconstruction: An Introduction to Theory and Method*. Oxford University Press 1995, pages 9–13

The following text discusses the controversial nature and status of the hypothetical forms reconstructed by comparative and internal reconstruction and indicates a way out of this controversy.

… one question … is fundamental to the whole enterprise of linguistic reconstruction: the status of reconstructed forms themselves. … [R]econstructed forms are initially hypothetical abstractions which result from attempts to relate attested linguistic forms, whether across different languages (as in the case of the Comparative Method) or within a single language (as in the case of Internal Reconstruction). But are we entitled to claim for such reconstructions the status of earlier linguistic forms? This controversy can be summed up in a confrontation between two views of reconstruction: the FORMULIST and the REALIST. The formulist view regards reconstructions merely as formulae which represent the various relationships within the data, while the less cautious realist view assumes that reconstructions can be taken to represent genuine historical forms of a real language, which happen not to have been recorded. …

Plausible arguments can be advanced in support of both the formulist and the realist positions. We must certainly acknowledge, for example, with the formulists, that reconstructions are abstractions which are dependent on the particular theoretical framework within which they are conceived, and this may lead us to conclude that they have no factual basis. But on the other hand *all* scientific constructs are abstract in this sense, and this does not necessarily prevent us from assuming the reality of the phenomena which they purport to describe. …

In spite of the apparent incompatibility of these two positions, there does, in fact, appear to be a way of resolving the conflict between them, which consists in recognizing that there are two distinct, though interrelated aspects of the reconstruction process: the APPLICATION OF THE METHODS on the one hand and the INTERPRETATION OF THE RESULTS on the other. … [T]he methods are formal procedures which produce particular results; these results can be taken as hypotheses about the historical facts; their historical validity will depend on other factors that are relevant to the process of interpretation, such as our knowledge of how languages change and of the principles on which languages are constructed and used.

> *Try to think of further arguments in support of either the formulist or the realist position.*

> *Is the comparison of reconstructed linguistic forms with the abstractions of natural science a valid one? Do, for example, subatomic particles have the same status as reconstructed linguistic forms? What would be the arguments for and against such a position?*

Text 3

ROGER LASS: *Historical Linguistics and Language Change.* Cambridge University Press 1997, pages 58–60

This text discusses the relationship between writing and speech in alphabetic writing systems and their importance as evidence for sound change.

For cultural reasons, as well as the fact that writing is learned later than speech, written language is generally more conservative than spoken. As we know (especially we English speakers), orthographies can remain unchanged for centuries, getting further and further away from the phonic substance they purport to represent. ... Sound changes (if they are recorded at all) typically first appear in the record as minor and variable deviations from earlier norms, and the usual working assumption is that the first occurrence of an innovative spelling indicates a long period of preceding change. ...

The previous discussions must of course be taken with numerous caveats. Perhaps the most important is that the closer in time a Roman-based orthography (say) is to its Latin source, the more likely its general norms are to reflect something like Latin ones. And conversely, the stronger the evidence for conventionalization and fixation of a tradition over a long period (during which we may expect considerable change), the less reliable such norms will be. ...

This seems to imply, curiously, that for interpreting spelling, it may be that the older a text is, the easier it is. On the one hand this could be a methodological copout (it's easier to interpret Old Icelandic as if it were Latin than Modern Icelandic); on the other, where there is good descriptive phonetic evidence ..., it's often relatively easy to establish the point of 'deflection' from the older norm type. But in the absence of metalinguistic commentary it seems safe (or often the only way) to assume a kind of Latin-based ... approach, i.e. to assume representational conservatism for older texts, at least as a starting point.

▷ *Modern English spelling is evidently far from reflecting the Latin norms mentioned in the text. What may be the reasons for this state of affairs?*

▷ *If modern English became extinct, and were only preserved in printed texts (for example, as the result of a global catastrophe), what difficulties would the reconstruction of its sound system pose to a historical linguist of, say, the twenty-second century?*

Text 4

LYLE CAMPBELL: *Historical Linguistics: An Introduction.*
Edinburgh University Press 1998, pages 188–9

In Chapter 2 we discussed comparative reconstruction and the family tree model, which rely heavily on the view that sound change is regular. This text discusses an alternative view on how languages develop and split, the so-called 'wave theory'.

Some scholars, many of them dialectologists, did not accept the Neogrammarian position that sound change is regular and exceptionless, but rather opposed this and the family-tree model. The slogan associated with opponents of the Neogrammarian position is *each word has its own history*. ... The alternative to the family-tree model which was put forward was the 'wave theory'. ... The 'wave theory' was intended to deal with changes due to contact among languages and dialects; in the wave model, changes were said to emanate from a centre as waves on a pond do when a stone is thrown into it, where waves from one centre of dispersion ... can cross or intersect outward-moving waves coming from other dispersion centres (started by other stones thrown into the water in other locations). Changes due to language contact (borrowing) were seen as analogous to successive waves crossing one another in different patterns. The dialectologists' slogan, that every word has its own history, reflects this thinking – a word's history might be the result of various influences from various directions, and these might be quite different from those involved in another word's history.

> *The proponents of the wave theory claim that 'each word has its own history'. Is such a view compatible with the basic assumptions of comparative and internal reconstruction as discussed in this chapter?*

Chapter 3
Vocabulary change

Text 5

HANS HENRICH HOCK *and* BRIAN D. JOSEPH: *Language History, Language Change, and Language Relationship: An*

Introduction to Historical and Comparative Linguistics.
Mouton de Gruyter 1996, pages 294–5

> *Cognates, i.e. words going back to a common source, are of basic importance for comparative reconstruction, but this relationship may be obscured through semantic change and sound change. Tracing the origin of words is the field of etymology, which is discussed in this text.*

The study of the origin of words is known as ETYMOLOGY. ... In a larger sense, etymology is concerned with the history of words, how they arise, the factors that have affected their ultimate shape and meaning, the semantic paths they have taken in their development through time, and so on. ... Far from being just a matter for trivial pursuits, etymology is in a real sense the basis of historical linguistics, for establishing the origin of a word is crucial to understanding the changes it has undergone and the factors that have influenced its development. Without a well-worked-out account of how *bead* could shift in meaning from an abstract meaning 'prayer' to a very concrete meaning 'small roundish glass or ceramic object' (through the use of rosary beads for counting prayers ...), we could not really establish its etymology, nor could we be sure about the effects of sound changes such as Grimm's Law in Germanic without first positing etymologies for various lexical items that connect them with cognate words in other languages (e.g. *father* as being from the same source as Latin *pater* ...). Thus, once a good many well-established cases are examined, working out the general principles that govern language change can be undertaken. And it all starts with etymology.

▷ *Consult an etymological dictionary such as the* Concise Oxford Dictionary *to find out where English* crayfish *comes from. Do you see any possible relation to English* crab?

▷ *Consider the following word meanings. Can you suggest how the modern meanings might have developed? (i) Middle English* flour *'flower; the best' > Modern English 'flour'; (ii)* fortune *'chance, good luck' > 'wealth'.*

Text 6

ELIZABETH CLOSS TRAUGOTT: 'On the rise of epistemic meanings in English: an example of subjectification in semantic change' in *Language* 65, 1989, pages 34–5

The following text proposes three tendencies or 'paths' of semantic change and thus tries to discover general principles of change similar to those established at the other linguistic levels.

PATHS OF SEMANTIC CHANGE ... [T]here are three closely-related tendencies, the first of which can feed the second and either of which can feed the third. ...

Tendency I: Meanings based in the external described situation > meanings based in the internal (evaluative/perceptual/cognitive) described situation.

This subsumes most of the familiar meaning changes known as pejoration and amelioration (e.g. *boor* 'farmer' > 'crude person'); a wide range of metaphorical extensions, most of them shifts from concrete to abstract; and the tendency identified by Sweetser 'to use vocabulary from the external (sociophysical) domain in speaking of the internal (emotional and psychological) domain' (1984: 56)—for example, early OE *felan* meant only 'touch'; it did not acquire a perceptual sense until late Old English. ...

Tendency II: Meanings based in the external or internal described situation > meanings based in the textual and meta-linguistic situation.

By 'textual situation' I mean the situation of text-construction. Examples include the development of lexical and morphological forms into connectives coding cohesion, as in the shift from *þa hwile þe* 'the time that' (coding an external described situation) > 'during' (coding the textual situation). By 'meta-linguistic situation' I mean the situation of performing a linguistic act. Examples include the shift from a mental-state to a speech-act verb meaning; for instance, in the early 1500's *observe* had the mental-verb meaning 'perceive (that)' (coding an internal described situation), and by 1605 it had come to be used as a speech-act verb in the sense 'state that' (coding the metalinguistic situation). ...

Tendency III: Meanings tend to become increasingly based in the speaker's subjective belief/attitude toward the proposition.

This tendency subsumes the shift of temporal to concessive *while* and a large number of other changes. Among them is the development of scalar particles such as *very*: borrowed in Middle English from Old French *verai* 'true' (a cognitive evaluation), in Early Modern English it became a scalar particle as in *the very height of her career* (a subjective evaluation). Tendency III also encompasses changes such as the development of the action verb *go* into a marker of immediate, planned future. ...

All three tendencies share one property: the later meanings presuppose a world not only of objects and states of affairs, but of values and of linguistic relations that cannot exist without language.

▷ *Under tendency I the writer subsumes amelioration and pejoration of meaning (see also Chapter 3). Do you think that this more general tendency I has more explanatory power than those two older concepts?*

▷ *The writer says that* þa hwile þe *in the sense of 'during' codes the textual situation. What do you think she means by this?*

▷ *The author claims that all 'the later meanings presuppose a world ... of values and of linguistic relations that cannot exist without language'. Can you give arguments for this view and some further examples exemplifying it?*

Text 7

PAUL J. HOPPER and ELIZABETH CLOSS TRAUGOTT: *Grammaticalization*. Cambridge University Press 1993, pages 6–7

The following text discusses the gradual nature of grammaticalization, a phenomenon which has attracted considerable interest recently.

Basic to work on grammaticalization is the concept of a "cline". ... From the point of view of change, forms do not shift abruptly from one category to another, but go through a series of gradual transitions, transitions that tend to be similar in type across languages. For example, a lexical noun like *back* that expresses a body part comes to stand for a spatial relationship in *in/at the back of*, and is susceptible to becoming an adverb, and perhaps eventually a preposition and even a case affix. Forms comparable to *back of* (*the house*) in English recur all over the world in different languages. The progression from lexical noun, to relational phrase, to adverb and preposition, and perhaps even to a case affix, is an example of what we mean by a cline.

The term "cline" itself has both historical and synchronic implications. From a historical perspective, a cline is a natural pathway along which forms evolve, a kind of linguistic "slippery slope" which guides the development of forms. Synchronically a cline can be thought of as a "continuum": an arrangement of forms along an imaginary line at one end of which is a fuller form of some kind, perhaps "lexical," and at the opposite end a compacted and reduced form, perhaps "grammatical."

▷ *Which of the three tendencies of semantic change discussed in Text 6 can be involved in grammaticalization?*

▷ *How far do English words like* because (< '*by cause*')*, instead illustrate the process of grammaticalization discussed here?*

Chapter 4
Grammatical change

Text 8
RUDI KELLER: *On Language Change: The Invisible Hand in Language.* Routledge 1994, pages 114–18

'Natural' approaches to general and historical linguistics have found enthusiastic supporters, but have also been severely criticized. This text acknowledges the insights gained through natural approaches, but is rather critical of its theoretical bases.

Research under the heading of 'naturalness' has achieved a host of interesting, sophisticated, and valuable results. Principles were formulated, historical drifts and trends were discovered, empirical observations were reorganised from the point of view of naturalness, and so on.

But so far, theoreticians of naturalness have failed to develop a consistent theory of naturalness. ...

Even the central concept of naturalness itself has not yet been provided with any binding explanation. No one has ever tried, to my knowledge, to integrate the concept of naturalness into a higher-order theoretical framework.

In other words, the controversial evaluation of the concept of naturalness is due to the fact that it has proved to be very productive and stimulating on the one hand, but on the other, that it was never theoretically elaborated, enabling it to resist sharp criticism. ...

Natural morphology, in the fields where it has been applied, has established that language change is directed; that is, it follows certain tendencies. Some of these tendencies are universal. They can come into conflict, which prevents the language system from reaching a standstill.

This statement is no mean result! But it provides no explanation. Exactly these tendencies and their universality are in need of explanation. ...

The concept of naturalness itself is normally defined in a circular, tautological way, but in any case very unclearly; that which is usual is unmarked is simpler is natural. ...

Apart from the tautological definition of naturalness, it is above all the lack of clarity of this concept which makes understanding difficult.

▷ *One point in the above criticism is the implied identity of the concepts 'natural', 'simple' and 'unmarked'. Do you think these necessarily coincide in language, or in any other social phenomenon?*

▷ *In some way the tendencies of semantic change discussed in Text 6 are also 'natural' tendencies. Do you think that these are open to the same kind of criticism as expressed in the present text?*

Text 9

ALICE C. HARRIS *and* LYLE CAMPBELL: *Historical Syntax in Cross-Linguistic Perspective.* Cambridge University Press 1995, pages 1–2

The following text advocates a cross-linguistic approach to historical syntax, i.e. an approach based on the comparison of data from a host of different languages, and is rather critical of research which relies too heavily on formal theories of grammar.

Recent work in diachronic syntax has been chiefly of three sorts: (1) studies of particular changes in individual languages; (2) research on specific kinds of change (e.g. word order change, grammaticalization); and (3) explorations of the diachronic implications of particular formal approaches to grammar, often given more to championing the particular theory of syntax than to actually accounting for linguistic changes. ... Rather than focusing on particular changes in individual languages, we investigate changes cross-linguistically. Rather than limiting attention to individual kinds of change (or single mechanisms of change), we establish commonalities in changes across languages and determine what mechanisms lie behind them and how they fit into the overall explanation of syntactic changes. ... While in principle the study of syntactic change should both inform and be informed by general linguistic theory, too often rigid devotion to a particular theory of syntax has limited rather than magnified insight into diachronic processes. Our findings clearly have relevance for general theories of syntax; however, we take as our starting point the actual changes themselves, rather than the predictions and constraints of any existing theory of syntax. ... Our interest is primarily in the nature of syntactic change, rather than in the form of the theory of such change ...

Specifically, in our study we have attempted (1) to investigate syntactic changes in a number of languages and language families, (2) to compare these to determine what are possible syntactic changes and what the commonly recurring types of changes are, and (3) to frame a general approach to syntactic change based on the results.

> *The authors say that their 'interest is primarily in the nature of syntactic change, rather than in the form of the theory of such change'. What do you think is the difference between an interest in syntactic change and an interest in the theory of such change?*

> *Try to work out the similarities between the approach advocated here and those presented in Texts 6 to 8 above. In what way do they all involve 'natural' changes?*

Text 10

ROBERT L. TRASK: *Historical Linguistics*. Arnold 1996, pages 139–42

In this chapter we discussed two mechanisms of syntactic change, namely reanalysis and word order changes connected with implicational universals. The following text discusses a further mechanism, namely shift of markedness.

There is another important pathway of syntactic change, called SHIFT OF MARKEDNESS. Languages typically have alternative constructions available for expressing ordinary and not-so-ordinary meanings. In English, for example, the ordinary (unmarked) word order is SVO, and we would therefore normally say *I can't recommend this book*, with SVO word order; this is the *unmarked form*. For special purposes, however, we can say instead *This book I can't recommend* – for example, when comparing the present book with other books. This construction with its abnormal object-subject-verb (OSV) word order, constitutes a *marked form*: an unusual form used only in certain special circumstances.

Now, suppose English-speakers were to begin using this marked form more frequently than at present. Suppose, ... that we began using ... the other construction, *I can't recommend this book*, only occasionally. What would be the result? First, the OSV construction, being used most of the time, would become the unmarked form, while the earlier SVO construction ... would become the marked form. We would therefore have a *shift of markedness* between the two forms. Moreover, since the two forms involve different word orders, ... English would therefore have undergone a change of basic word order from SVO to OSV.

This has not happened in English, of course, but precisely this sort of development has occurred in the histories of a number of other languages. ...

In a markedness shift, it is not always the case that a formerly marked form becomes unmarked and vice versa. The opposite may happen: the marked form may become even more highly marked, possibly to the point at which it disappears from the language, or nearly so. For a thousand years English has had two competing forms for constructing sentences involving prepositions and WH-words. The first is represented by examples like

To whom did you give it? … ; the second is illustrated by *Who did you give it to? …* The first form has been the marked form for centuries, but there is no sign that it might take over from the second. Quite the contrary: the first, marked, form has been steadily declining in frequency for generations. Today it is probably entirely confined to the formal writing of a minority of speakers and to the careful speech of an even smaller minority … and it may eventually disappear completely.

▷ *The writer says that both 'This book I can't recommend' and 'To whom did you give it?' are marked forms, though they evidently represent two very different forms of markedness. Can you tell in regard to which feature or dimension these two sentences are marked?*

▷ *How far does the above-discussed hypothetical case of a shift of word order have anything in common with the word order shifts related with implicational universals as discussed in Chapter 4?*

Chapter 5

Sound change

Text 11

WINFRED P. LEHMANN: *Historical Linguistics: An Introduction* (3rd edn.). Routledge 1992, pages 205–6

In Chapter 5 we discussed phonemic change in terms of whole segments, i.e. phonemes, as well as in terms of phonological features. Generative phonology, on the other hand, describes sound change as change in the rules of grammar. Some major types of rule change are introduced in the following extract.

[Trubetzkoy, the founding father of phonemic theory] regarded phonological elements and processes as rules. The view was continued by generative linguistics, so that in their treatment change consists of modifications of rules in the competence of speakers. Specific changes, then, have been labeled by the effect on rules.

    When sound change involves innovations, the event is

described as RULE ADDITION. The changes described in Grimm's law ... and in the Great Vowel Shift are examples of rule addition.

When, on the other hand, the application of a rule is no longer maintained, the event is referred to as RULE LOSS. ... A third type of change is ascribed to RULE REORDERING. Two languages or dialects may exhibit the same rules, but the rules may differ in order. ...

Besides reinterpreting sound change, and the results of sound change in this way, grammarians with a generative point of view have introduced terms for rules that can be related to other rules. For example, if a rule describes changes that expand the scope of subsequent rules, the earlier rule is labeled a FEEDING RULE, and the group of rules is said to stand in a FEEDING RELATIONSHIP. ... But languages also undergo changes that conflict with the pattern of earlier changes. Such changes are referred to as BLEEDING RULES; BLEEDING RELATIONSHIP, then, results in diminution of scope.

In order to understand the publications that deal with sound change as rules change, students must be aware of their basis, and of their difference from earlier descriptions and historical treatments. The use of rules is not new, for ... rules have been used since the days of Grimm. ... Rather, it is the identification of linguistic phenomena through rules, and the discussion of linguistic changes as rule changes that are characteristic of this approach.

▷ *Phonological rules are formalized ways of expressing linguistic regularities. Do you think that such rules provide explanations of change which are superior to traditional explanations, or are they only elegant descriptive devices?*

▷ *What do you think is the difference between 'the use of rules' and 'the identification of linguistic phenomena through rules'? (Cf. also the discussion of 'application of methods' and 'interpretation of the results' in Text 2.)*

Text 12
ROBERT J. JEFFERS *and* ILSE LEHISTE: *Principles and Methods for Historical Linguistics*. MIT Press 1979, pages 14–15

In Chapter 5 we concentrated on changes in the segmental sound units of languages. This text looks at changes in prosodic features and their possible interaction with segmental sounds. (Many linguists would disagree with including 'quantity' under the concept of 'prosodic feature'. However, this does not affect the main argument of this passage, which is the interaction between quantity and stress.)

Not only may phonological change affect the system of segmental sounds, but the prosodic system of a language may undergo various types of changes, which, in turn, may affect the segmental system. Each of the three prosodic features—quantity, tone, and stress—may be involved in the change. Languages may lose an original quantity opposition or develop a new one; languages may lose or acquire distinctive tone; formerly free and distinctive stress may become fixed and acquire the value of a boundary signal, or stress shift patterns may develop that acquire linguistic function. All these prosodic changes may interact with segmental changes, either resulting from a change in the segmental system or producing a change in the segmental system as a result of the change in the suprasegmental system.

The following example illustrates some possibilities. It is well known that Latin at one time possessed a quantity opposition in vowels; words like *populus* 'people' and *pōpulus* 'poplar' constituted minimal pairs. Developing into the various Romance languages, the parent language lost the original quantity opposition, replacing it by a system involving a larger number of vowels differing in phonetic quality. Latin started with a basic system of five vowels, which could be either long or short: *ī, i; ē, e; ā, a; ō, o;* and *ū, u*. At an intermediate stage (often referred to as Vulgar Latin), the length opposition was lost; long *ī* and *ū* continued as [i] and [u], short *i* merged with long *ē* as [e] and short *u* merged with long *ō* as [o]; short *e* became phonetic [ɛ] and short *o* developed into [ɔ]; the length distinction between *ā* and *a* disappeared, leaving a seven-vowel system without a length opposition. Individual Romance languages have undergone further developments; Italian, for example, shows diphthongs in words that, in Latin, contained short *e* and short *o* in open syllables. ...

The Italian stressed vowels in open syllables are phonetically longer than unstressed vowels. Note that the development of diphthongs from short vowels implies that the loss of the quantity opposition must have evolved by way of lengthening of short vowels rather than through a reduction of the duration of long vowels. In Latin, vowel length was independent of stress; in Italian, stress conditions the length of vowels, and vowel length may be considered a stress cue. The change in one supra-segmental feature (quantity) has brought about a restructuring of several different aspects of the phonological system.

▷ *The phonological changes discussed in Chapter 5 focused on sounds and phonemes, i.e. on segmental units. How far does this text lead us to rethink some of the assumptions made in Chapter 5?*

▷ *How far do the vowel systems of Latin, French, and Italian differ typologically, i.e. in regard to a specific feature which might be used for classifying these languages into different groups? (Consult also Chapter 5.)*

Chapter 6

Language contact

Text 13

OLGA FISCHER: 'Syntactic change and borrowing: the case of the accusative-and-infinitive construction in English' in Marinel Gerritsen and Dieter Stein (eds.): *Internal and External Factors in Syntactic Change*. Mouton de Gruyter 1992, pages 17–19

In the majority of cases it is unproblematic to decide whether a specific word has been borrowed from another language. Syntactic borrowing, on the other hand, is much harder to detect and it is often impossible to be absolutely certain about it.

In the history of practically every language we come across syntactic constructions that were once foreign to that language but which were (or are) common constructions in other languages with which the language in question was in contact. In studying such syntactic innovations linguists may, and often have, come to the conclusion that a change was brought about by "syntactic borrowing". Cases in point in the history of English are the use of the absolute participle ... in imitation of the Latin *ablativus absolutus* ... ; the employment of subjectless relatives in Middle English (ascribed to French ...); the development of periphrastic *do* (due to Celtic ...), etc. In most of these presumed cases of syntactic borrowing, however, there is hardly a consensus of opinion on whether the new construction is indeed caused by borrowing or by some other factor or factors or a combination of these. ... It seems clear that syntactic borrowing is no easy matter to establish, and that in many, if not most, cases, other factors are at least co-responsible for the introduction of a new construction. ...

It almost goes without saying that for all kinds of borrowing (except to a certain extent lexical borrowing) a certain length and intensity of contact is crucial. ... As far as English is concerned, Latin, Celtic, Scandinavian, and French seem to fulfill these particular conditions and are, not surprisingly, often mentioned as possible causes/sources for changes that have taken place in the periods relevant for these contacts. ... A distinction that seems particularly relevant is whether the contact was of an oral or a written nature. ...

[A] problem involving the recognition of syntactic borrowing is the question of how one can distinguish whether a syntactical point of agreement between two languages is due to influence or to parallel development. Blatt (1957: 38ff.) has set up a number of criteria which may be of help in settling this point: i) Does the new construction fit the syntactic system of the adopting language at all or is it quite alien to it? ii) Has the new construction supplanted another (indigenous) construction (in which case Blatt thinks foreign influence is more likely)? iii) What is the frequency of the construction in translated/learned texts as compared to original literature?

> *The author says that for borrowing to take place 'a certain length and intensity of contact is crucial' except 'to a certain extent' in the case of lexical borrowing. Why do you think lexical borrowing may be an exception?*

> *All the above-mentioned languages, Latin, Celtic, Scandinavian and French, are, though to a varying degree of closeness, also genetically related to English. Do you see a way of distinguishing between constructions inherited from the common ancestor and those due to borrowing?*

Text 14

TERRY CROWLEY: *An Introduction to Historical Linguistics* (3rd edn.). Oxford University Press 1997, page 197

This text discusses a special type of language contact, namely those cases where one of the languages in contact is given up by its speakers, but leaves traces, a so-called substratum, in the surviving language.

The *substratum* theory of linguistic change involves the idea that if people migrate into an area and their language is acquired by the original inhabitants of the area, then any changes in the language can be put down to the influence of the original language. ...

It is well known that a person's first language will to some extent influence the way in which that person will speak a second language. We can all recognise foreign accents in our own language. It is quite easy to tell whether someone is a native speaker of English, or whether their first language is French, German, Chinese, or Samoan. While Black Americans today have English as their first language, it is often possible to point to features of the English spoken by Blacks which are not present in the English spoken by Whites. Some of these features ... have been put down to the features of the original languages of the African slaves who were first transported to America hundreds of years ago. It may turn out that these features do not derive from African languages at all, but if, on the other hand, this argument turns out to be correct, then this would be an example of how substratum has influenced the direction that one variety of a language has taken.

The problem with the substratum explanation of language change is that it is sometimes used to explain changes in languages where the supposed substratum language (or languages) have ceased to exist. The influence of the substratum in such cases can be neither proved nor disproved. One example of substratum influence that is often quoted involves the history of French. ... France is now split into two major dialect areas between the north and the south. Some scholars have suggested that this split corresponds to an earlier split in the original Celtic language [spoken there before the time of the Roman Empire] and that these differences were carried over into the Latin the spoke when they switched languages. While this is a perfectly plausible theory, since the original Celtic language no longer survives in France, it can neither be proved nor disproved.

▷ *Can you think of reasons why substratum features should survive in a language for centuries or even millennia?*

▷ *The author points out that the Celtic origin of the French dialect split 'can be neither proved nor disproved'. Do you think that it is legitimate to work with a theory which cannot be falsified?*

Text 15

MARK SEBBA: *Contact Languages: Pidgin and Creoles.* Macmillan 1997, pages 111–12

In the process of creolization, the linguistic structure of the former pidgin develops on all linguistic levels so that the emerging creole can function as a fully fledged language. In this process, grammaticalization may play a major role, as in the following syntactic developments in Tok Pisin, which has developed via a stable pidgin into a creole.

[G]rammatical categories such as tense, aspect and modality in pidgins are often marked by what in the lexifier [i.e. the language from which most of the vocabulary of the pidgin derives] are content words—for example, adverbs and verbs. In the early stages of a pidgin, it is likely that these markers still have the status of content words; ...

As the communicative complexity of a pidgin increases, content words (i.e. those which bear independent meaning) may be re-analysed to take on a grammatical function. This process is called GRAMMATICALISATION. Naturally, it is more likely to affect those aspects of the pidgin grammar which are most impoverished at the outset, so the marking of tense/modality/aspect (TMA) is an area where grammaticalisation often occurs.

We mentioned ... the Tok Pisin future marker *bai*, derived from English 'by-and-by' ... We have enough historical documentation to be able to chart the different stages of this word in Tok Pisin. According to Sankoff and Laberge (1974), in its earliest stages, *baimbai* functioned as a sentence adverbial meaning 'afterwards' or 'later'. It later became a preverbal particle, and subsequently a verb prefix indicating future. At the same time, it has undergone phonological change: from *baimbai* to *bəmbai* to *bai* to *bə*. This kind of grammatical re-analysis going hand in hand with phonological reduction is typical of grammaticalisation as a process. As an item alters in status from content word to grammatical morpheme, it loses much of its phonetic 'baggage' as well.

Given that a pidgin starts out with minimal grammar, its grammatical development along the developmental continuum will largely consist of developing new and more elaborate grammatical categories, complete with the appropriate marking. The means whereby this takes place is largely through the grammaticalisation of existing content words.

▷ As discussed in Chapter 4 and Text 7, grammaticalization is also an important mechanism of linguistic change in 'normal' languages. Do the changes in the TMA systems of Tok Pisin and of English (cf. Chapter 4) show any similarities with regard to grammaticalization?

▷ Is the use of forms such as 'baimbai' etc. in Tok Pisin a sign that Tok Pisin is 'corrupt' English? Try to give reasons for your view.

▷ Do you see any relation between the substratum theory discussed in Text 14 and the processes of pidginization and creolization? (Cf. also Chapter 6.)

Chapter 7

How and why do languages change?

Text 16

JAMES MILROY: *Linguistic Variation and Change: On the Historical Sociolinguistics of English*. Blackwell 1992, pages 10–11

Milroy establishes three principles of a speaker-centred social explanation of linguistic change. Principles 1 and 2 emphasize that language use as well as the description of language structure are only possible in relation to the social and situational contexts of language. This text discusses

Principle 3, which stresses the importance of language maintenance for a theory of linguistic change.

Principle 3 In order to account for differential patterns of change at particular times and places, we need first to take account of those factors that tend to maintain language states and resist change.

This is closely related to the *actuation problem*, ... and the emphasis on language maintenance is the most salient difference between the way I have approached historical linguistic change and the approach of most other historical linguists. ... It gives rise to a number of consequential differences in approach. Historical linguists do not generally describe patterns of *maintenance*: they tend to focus on those things that are known to have changed and ignore those things that have not, and they can often explicate historical changes very elegantly without any reference at all to the social embedding of the changes concerned. What strikes me as important here, however, is the fact that if we focus exclusively on change and ignore maintenance, these non-social procedures can be quite easily justified: we can indeed propose sophisticated descriptions and highly constrained theories of linguistic change, without taking any account of social factors, and this is frequently done. However, if we pose the more basic question why some forms and varieties remain stable while others change, we cannot avoid reference to society. ...

If we are interested in how language states can remain stable and how speech communities *resist* change, we have almost no alternative but to take account of social factors.

> Do you think that language change and language maintenance are basically two sides of the same coin?

> The author says that if we consider language maintenance as well as change, 'we cannot avoid reference to society'. Do you agree?

> The writer states that 'to take account of those factors that tend to maintain language states and resist change ... is closely related to the actuation problem'. Why do you think this is so?

Text 17

LYLE CAMPBELL: *Historical Linguistics: An Introduction.*
Edinburgh University Press 1998, page 199

*In Chapter 7 we discussed the concept of lexical diffusion, the
hypothesis that sound change spreads gradually through the
vocabulary. This text from a recent introduction expresses a
critical attitude towards this hypothesis and suggests alternative explanations for the spread of sound change.*

[The theory of lexical diffusion] constitutes a different outlook on
the transition problem. It should be kept in mind, however, that in
spite of strong claims that lexical diffusion is a more basic
mechanism by which change is transmitted than Neogrammarian
regularity, very few cases of lexical diffusion have actually been
reported, and most of these are doubtful.

While several cases have been analysed as lexical diffusion,
most mainstream historical linguists have not been convinced. ...
On closer scrutiny, most of these cases prove not to be real
instances of lexical diffusion but to be more reliably explained by
other means. Often it turns out that the phonetic conditioning
environments are quite complex—important phonetic environments were missed in several of the cases for which lexical
diffusion was claimed. Detailed studies of the same cases by
people aware of the claims for lexical diffusion have found
sounds behaving regularly in change in these environments and
no evidence of lexical conditioning. When the environments are
understood, Neogrammarian regularity is what was behind the
changes and not lexical diffusion after all. In the examples from
the history of Chinese, which had been influential support for
lexical diffusion, it turns out that the extent of borrowing from
literary Chinese into the varieties of Chinese studied was vastly
more extensive than originally thought.

▷ *The author claims that factors such as borrowing, analogy
and erroneous analysis can equally well account for irregular
forms. Do you think that the case of 'yod-dropping' discussed
in this chapter can be explained in this way?*

▷ *Do you see a way in which apparently regular sound change
can be reconciled with the hypothesis of lexical diffusion?*

▷ In Text 4 the wave theory was discussed as an alternative to the Neogrammarian position. Do you see any relation between the wave theory and lexical diffusion?

Text 18

JANET HOLMES: *An Introduction to Sociolinguistics.*
Longman 1992, pages 231–4

In Chapter 7 we mentioned the role of the social variable 'sex' (or gender) in language change. This text discusses this complex issue in more detail, using research in a Belfast working-class community. It seems that the type of networks and social contacts in which speakers interact may be more important for a particular change than their sex.

Differences in women's and men's speech are another source of variation which can result in linguistic change. Sometimes it is women who are the innovators, leading a linguistic change, and sometimes it is men. In general, women tend to introduce the prestige forms, whereas men tend to lead changes in the opposite direction, introducing new vernacular forms. ...

... These generalisations account for differences in women's and men's role in relation to language change in a variety of communities. But there are at least two types of exception to these patterns. First, women sometimes introduce vernacular changes into a community, and, secondly, there are communities where women are not leading linguistic change in any direction. ... [T]he Clonard women are introducing into their community a speech feature which they are imitating from the more prestigious Ballymacarrett community. Although this is a change towards the vernacular not towards the standard dialect, it is a vernacular form used by an admired group within the Belfast context. ...

... These women had also developed work and leisure patterns which resembled those of traditionally male groups. So the introduction of vernacular forms into their community by these young women reflected their daily networks and broader range of contacts through their work. It also indicates the importance of solidarity in favouring and consolidating vernacular forms in the speech of any group, male or female, who both work and play together.

Finally, the generalisation about women leading change towards the standard dialect applies only where women play some role in public life. In Iran and India, for instance, it has been found that women's speech does not follow the western pattern. In these places the status of women is relatively fixed and there is no motivation for them to lead linguistic change. ... In these societies women do not lead linguistic innovation in any direction.

▷ *Judging from the above text and the discussion of socio linguistic explanations of change in this chapter, which social variables do you think are the most important ones in linguistic change?*

▷ *How far does this text provide arguments for the frequently made distinction between (biological) sex and (social) gender?*

Text 19
ANTHONY FOX: *Linguistic Reconstruction: An Introduction to Theory and Method.* Oxford University Press 1995, pages 250–1

In Chapters 2, 4, and 7, we have referred to the importance of linguistic typology and language universals for historical linguistics. This text discusses the relation between the synchronic and the diachronic implications of universals and typology.

Language universals and typology are in the first instance *synchronic* concepts, which relate to the nature and form of language itself. Nevertheless, both universal and typological principles have potential diachronic applications, the nature of these applications depending very much on how we view the relationship between the synchronic and diachronic dimension of language. ... Thus, if we assume universal and typological factors to be constraints on synchronic systems, structures, or grammars, then they are relevant for language change inasmuch as they impose limitations on the states out of or into which the transitions may lead. Thus, if languages have certain universal properties, or must conform to particular typological con straints, then it is clear that no change can take place which would result in a language state which lacks these universal properties or violates these constraints. In the case of typological change itself similar principles apply. If language types are defined in terms of combinations of particular values for a certain set of parameters, linked by implicational universals (e.g. the ordering of verb and object and the ordering of adjective and noun), then a change in the value of one of these parameters may entail a change in the other, which ensures that the language does not have an inadmissible combination of values in the resulting language state.

From this point of view, therefore, universals and typologies are essentially synchronic attributes of languages, which influence language change to the extent that they determine the form of the successive language states which result from this change.

▷ *The author states that universal and typological factors 'are relevant for language change inasmuch as they impose limitations on the states out of or into which the transitions may lead'. Does this say anything about the limitations on the transitions between language states, i.e. on the process of language change itself?*

▷ *Are the conclusions drawn in the text also valid if universals are not seen as absolute, but rather as statistical preferences or tendencies, as proposed by many linguists?*

Chapter 8
Postscript: further developments

Text 20
TERRENCE W. DEACON: *The Symbolic Species: The Co-Evolution of Language and the Human Brain*. Penguin 1997, pages 110–15

This text views language change 'in evolutionary terms' as resulting from adaptations in the processes of reproduction and selection in language acquisition. The connection between language acquisition and change is, however, not seen as being due to an in-built Universal Grammar, but rather to principles of copying and natural selection.

[L]anguages are far more like living organisms than like mathematical proofs. The most basic principle guiding their design is not communicative utility but reproduction—theirs and ours. So, the proper tool for analyzing language structure may not be to discover how best to model them as axiomatic rule systems but rather to study them the way we study organism structure: in evolutionary terms. Languages are social and cultural entities that have evolved with respect to the forces of selection imposed by human users.

The structure of a language is under intense selection because in its reproduction from generation to generation, it must pass through a narrow bottleneck: children's minds. ... Language operations that can be learned quickly and easily by children will tend to get passed on to the next generation more effectively and more intact than those that are difficult to learn. So, languages should change through history in ways that tend to conform to children's expectations; those that employ a more kid-friendly logic should come to outnumber and replace those that don't. ...

If, as linguists often point out, grammars appear illogical and quirky in their design, it may only be because we are comparing them to inappropriate models and judging their design according to functional criteria that are less critical than we think. Instead of approximating an imaginary ideal of communicative power and efficiency, or following formulae derived from an alleged set of innate mental principles, language structures may simply reflect the selection pressures that have shaped their reproduction.

In some ways it is helpful to imagine language as an independent life form that colonizes and parasitizes human brains, using them to reproduce. ...

In the case of language and human beings ... we should not be surprised to find complex human adaptations to language on the one hand, whose purpose is to ensure that language is successfully replicated and passed from host to host, and language adaptation to children on the other, whose purpose is to make language particularly "infective" as early as possible in human development. Modern humans need the language parasite in order to flourish and reproduce, just as much as it needs humans to reproduce. ... The adaptation of the parasite to its hosts, particularly children provides the basis for a theory of prescient language learning. ...

The key to understanding language learnability ... lies in a process that seems otherwise far remote from the microcosm of toddlers and caretakers—language change. ... [T]his process is crucial to understanding how the child can learn a language that on the surface appears impossibly complex and poorly taught. The mechanisms driving language change at the sociocultural level are also responsible for everyday language learning.

▷ *The writer says that 'languages ... that employ a more kid-friendly logic should come to outnumber and replace those that don't'. Is this evolutionary view compatible with that of an innate Universal Grammar presented in Chapter 7?*

▷ *The writer refers to language as a parasitic system, with humans adapting to language as well as language adapting to humans to facilitate mutual replication. Do you think that this is merely a nice metaphor or does language really function like biological parasitic systems?*

Text 21

RONALD WARDHAUGH: *An Introduction to Sociolinguistics* (3rd edn.). Blackwell 1998, pages 347; 360–1

Sociolinguists generally distinguish two types of language planning, namely 'status planning', i.e. measures to change the official status of a language, and 'corpus planning', though the two are clearly interrelated. The following text discusses some aspects of corpus planning in Tok Pisin.

Corpus planning seeks to develop a variety of a language or a language, usually to standardize it, that is, to provide it with the means for serving every possible language function in society. Consequently, corpus planning may involve such matters as the development of an orthography, new sources of vocabulary, dictionaries, and a literature, together with the deliberate cultivation of new uses so that the language may extend its use into such areas as government, education, and trade. ... [347]

Papua New Guinea has three official languages which are all second languages to the vast majority of its people: Hiri Motu, Tok Pisin, and English. ... Of the three, Tok Pisin is becoming more and more the first language of many young people, particularly city dwellers. ... Tok Pisin is a pidgin-based language; consequently, it must be developed to meet the various new needs it must serve. Such growth is not without its difficulties. One particular development that has met with negative reaction from a number of linguists is that, for pragmatic reasons, vocabulary expansion has taken place through large-scale borrowing from English, rather than through the exploitation of native resources, e.g., words such as *amenmen*, *ekspendisa*, *eleksen*, *komisin*, *mosin*, *praim minista*, *privilij*, and *spika*. English exerts a powerful influence on Tok Pisin. Anglicized varieties of the language may show not only borrowings of English words but also the occasional English plural -*s*, use of English subordination patterns and the English counting system, and so on. ... Tok Pisin is still so distinct from English that there is no evidence of a continuum between Tok Pisin and English. However, there is a real danger that a continuum could develop with Standard English at the 'top' and local varieties of Tok Pisin at the 'bottom', much as in Jamaica ... , with all the attendant problems.

Tok Pisin has also developed a number of sub-varieties, particularly in urban areas, so that it is now not as uniform as it once was. There is some risk that, without a deliberate effort to standardize the language, it will not remain as efficient a lingua franca as it has been. Deliberate language planning rather than *ad hoc* developments seem increasingly necessary. It is also in the country's interest that the variety that should be developed is the rural variety, the less Anglicized, more stable variety recognized by the people themselves as the 'good' variety of Tok Pisin. [360–1]

▷ *From a purely linguistic point of view, lexical and structural borrowing (see Chapter 6) and the development of a dialect continuum are natural phenomena. Give arguments for and against attempts to counteract this development by measures of corpus planning, i.e. conscious interference, in the case of Tok Pisin.*

SECTION 3
References

The following references are classified into introductory (marked
■□□), more advanced and more technical (marked ■■□), and
specialized, very demanding (marked ■■■).

Chapter 1
Language change as a matter of fact

■□□
JEAN AITCHISON: *Language Change: Progress or Decay?*
(2nd edn.). Cambridge University Press 1991

An excellent introduction, with particular emphasis on the social
causes of linguistic change. Particularly suited for the reader
without prior knowledge in linguistics.

■□□
ROBERT L.TRASK: *Historical Linguistics*. Arnold 1996

A well-written and up-to-date introduction, which is well suited
as follow-up reading to the present book. Chapter 1 covers
similar topics to those in the present Chapter 1.

Chapter 2
Reconstructing the past: data and evidence

■□□
TERRY CROWLEY: *An Introduction to Historical Linguistics*
(3rd edn.). Oxford University Press 1997

Chapter 5 of this introduction discusses Comparative Reconstruction, mainly using data from Polynesian languages, and Chapter 6 Internal Reconstruction. Chapter 13 is devoted to 'Cultural Reconstruction', a subject only briefly dealt with in the present book.

■■□

ANTHONY FOX: *Linguistic Reconstruction: An Introduction to Theory and Method*. Oxford University Press 1995

This is an up-to-date account of the theoretical bases and methodology of comparative and internal reconstruction.

■■■

ROGER LASS: *Historical Linguistics and Language Change*. Cambridge University Press 1997

This is a stimulating book for the more advanced student, critically discussing the underlying assumptions of historical linguistics and some of their philosophical implications.

■■□

WINFRED P. LEHMANN: *Historical Linguistics: An Introduction* (3rd edn.). Routledge 1992

Chapters 7 and 8 of this standard introduction discuss comparative and internal reconstruction using extensive material from the Indo-European languages, especially the Germanic language family.

Chapter 3
Vocabulary change

■□□

HANS HENRICH HOCK and BRIAN D. JOSEPH: *Language History, Language Change, and Language Relationship: An Introduction to Historical and Comparative Linguistics*. Mouton de Gruyter 1996

This is a comprehensive introduction for the non-specialist Chapters 7 to 9 deal extensively with 'change in the lexicon'.

■□□

FRANCIS KATAMBA: *English Words*. Routledge 1994

A well-written and accessible introduction to the English vocabulary. Though adopting a predominantly synchronic perspective, it also incorporates information on diachronic aspects, including many of the topics treated here in Chapter 3.

Chapter 4
Grammatical change

■■□

STEPHEN R. ANDERSON: 'Morphological change' in Frederick J. Newmeyer (ed.): *Linguistics: The Cambridge Survey I: Linguistic Theory: Foundations*. Cambridge University Press 1988, pages 324–62

This is a good survey of morphological change for the more advanced reader, highlighting the relationship between phonology, morphology, and syntax in morphological change, with examples from a wide range of languages.

■■□

RAIMO ANTTILA: *Historical and Comparative Linguistics* (2nd edn.). Benjamins 1989

Chapter 5 of this well-established handbook gives a detailed description of analogy and the interplay between analogy and sound change. Chapter 16 discusses morphological typology.

■■■

ALICE C. HARRIS and LYLE CAMPBELL: *Historical Syntax in Cross-Linguistic Perspective*. Cambridge University Press 1995

This book for the advanced reader develops a cross-linguistic approach to historical syntax, i.e. an approach based on the comparison of data from a host of languages. On the basis of these data, the authors try to establish universals of syntactic change.

■■□

PAUL J. HOPPER and ELIZABETH CLOSS TRAUGOTT:
Grammaticalization. Cambridge University Press 1993

This is a comprehensive overview of the processes involved in grammaticalization, with extensive illustrations from English and a wide variety of other languages.

■■□

APRIL M.S. MCMAHON: *Understanding Language Change.*
Cambridge University Press 1994

Chapter 4 on morphological change deals with analogy and also gives a brief survey on natural morphology. Chapter 5 critically evaluates the earlier and later versions of Lightfoot's theory of syntactic change. Chapter 6 discusses typology, word order, and grammaticalization.

Chapter 5
Sound change

■■□

LYLE CAMPBELL: *Historical Linguistics: An Introduction.*
Edinburgh University Press 1998

Chapter 2 of this recent textbook provides a detailed description of phonetic and phonemic change, illustrated by numerous examples from both Indo-European and non-Indo-European language families, including American Indian languages.

■■■

HANS HENRICH HOCK: *Principles of Historical Linguistics*
(2nd edn.). Mouton de Gruyter 1991

Chapters 3–8 of this comprehensive handbook offer a detailed, sometimes rather technical survey of the types of phonetic and phonemic change, including structural and functional aspects of phonemic change.

■■□

PAUL KIPARSKY: 'Phonological change' in Frederick J.
Newmeyer (ed.): *Linguistics: The Cambridge Survey I:*

Linguistic Theory: Foundations. Cambridge University Press 1988, pages 363–415

A good critical overview of the main theoretical approaches to phonological change, from the Neogrammarians to the present.

Chapter 6
Language contact

■□□

DAVID CRYSTAL: *Language Death*. Cambridge University Press 2000

This book is a passionate plea for the preservation of endangered languages, which are discussed in some detail. Its focus is on the social and sociolinguistic aspects of language death, while it neglects the purely linguistic aspects of the process.

■■□

SARAH GREY THOMASON and TERRENCE KAUFMAN: *Language Contact, Creolization, and Genetic Linguistics*. University of California Press 1988

This is a comprehensive though sometimes controversial account of language change resulting from language contact. Among the numerous case studies the thorough discussion and refutation of the hypothesis that Middle English is basically a creole deserves particular mention.

■■□

ILSE LEHISTE: *Lectures on Language Contact*. MIT Press 1988

This is a good, concise introduction to the most important language contact phenomena.

■□□

MARK SEBBA: *Contact Languages: Pidgins and Creoles*. Macmillan 1997

A well-written and up-to-date account of all relevant aspects of pidgin and creole languages. Chapters 4 and 5 deal with questions of creolization and supply extensive linguistic data.

■■□
PETER TRUDGILL: *Dialects in Contact*. Blackwell 1986

This is a sociolinguistic study on linguistic change due to dialect contact. Though the focus is on varieties of English, other languages are also extensively referred to.

Chapter 7
How and why do languages change?

■□□
LAURIE BAUER: *Watching English Change: An Introduction to the Study of Linguistic Change in Standard Englishes in the Twentieth Century*. Longman 1994

This is a highly readable account of linguistic change in contemporary standard varieties of English, which also presents the main issues of a variationist approach to linguistic change.

■□□
RUDI KELLER: *On Language Change: The Invisible Hand in Language*. Routledge 1994 (German original 1990)

Starting from the assumption that language is a phenomenon of the 'third kind', i.e. neither 'natural' nor 'artificial', the author develops a hypothesis of language change as resulting from the working of the 'invisible hand'. An intellectually challenging book written in a style accessible to the non-specialist.

■■□
WILLIAM LABOV: *Sociolinguistic Patterns*. University of Pennsylvania Press 1972 (British edition Blackwell 1978)

This classic book provides a survey of the Labovian approach to language change up to the 1970s. It also contains the well-known studies on Martha's Vineyard and the New York department stores.

■■■
WILLIAM LABOV: *Principles of Linguistic Change Vol. 1: Internal Factors*. Blackwell 1994

This volume provides a detailed discussion of the internal factors that govern linguistic change. On the basis of extensive empirical research on current changes in English, it presents the central aspects of phonological change, such as chain shifts, mergers, splits and the regularity hypothesis. One of the most important contributions to the field in the last decade.

■■□

JAMES MILROY: *Linguistic Variation and Change: On the Historical Sociolinguistics of English*. Blackwell 1992

This book discusses historical and current changes in English within a social model of change. Based on the theory of social networks, it centres on the role of the speaker and their social ties for an explanation of linguistic change.

Chapter 8
Postscript: further developments

■■□

DONNA CHRISTIAN: 'Language planning: the view from linguistics' in Frederick J. Newmeyer (ed.): *Linguistics: The Cambridge Survey IV: Language: The Socio-Cultural Context*. Cambridge University Press 1988, pages 193–209

This chapter offers a brief survey on the main issues of language planning, with particular emphasis on the contributions made by (socio)linguistics.

■□□

JAMES MILROY and LESLEY MILROY: *Authority in Language: Investigating Standard English* (3rd edn.). Routledge 1999

This well-written book considers both the historical and the social aspects of standardization.

■■□

ANDREAS H. JUCKER (ed.): *Historical Pragmatics*. Benjamins 1995

An interesting collection of articles on this young discipline. Though most provide data-orientated case studies, theoretical issues are also addressed. Most contributions are accessible to the non-specialist.

Apart from the above titles, reference should also be made to the relevant entries in encyclopedias on linguistics:

■■■

R.E. ASHER (ed.): *The Encyclopedia of Language and Linguistics*. (10 volumes) Pergamon 1994

■■□

WILLIAM BRIGHT (ed.): *International Encyclopedia of Linguistics*. (4 volumes) Oxford University Press 1992

■□□

DAVID CRYSTAL: *The Cambridge Encyclopedia of Language* (2nd edn.). Cambridge University Press 1997

The following are useful dictionaries of linguistic terms:

■□□

DAVID CRYSTAL: *A Dictionary of Linguistics and Phonetics* (4th edn.). Blackwell 1997

■■□

ROBERT L. TRASK: *The Dictionary of Historical and Comparative Linguistics*. Edinburgh University Press 2000

■■□

HADUMOD BUSSMANN: *Routledge Dictionary of Language and Linguistics*. Routledge 1996

SECTION 4
Glossary

Page references to Section 1 (Survey) are given at the end of each entry.

actuation The beginning of a change. [77]

affixation The formation of a new word by adding a prefix or suffix to a base, e.g. **unhappy**, *happiness*. [26]

agglutinating language A language in which words consist of **morphemes** which are formally neatly separable and each have a single meaning, such as Turkish, Japanese, *See also* **inflecting language, isolating language**. [35]

amelioration of meaning The process whereby a word loses its negative or unpleasant meaning, or improves a neutral meaning, e.g. *marshal* (originally 'keeper of horses'). [31]

analogy A process by which a form or pattern becomes more similar to another (usually more regular) one, e.g. *mouses* for *mice*, in analogy with regular plurals in -(*e*)*s*. [37]

analytic language A language in which the syntactic and semantic relationships between words are predominantly expressed by separate grammatical words, e.g. *more difficult* (vs. synthetic *heavier*); *the house of my friend* (vs. synthetic *my friend's house*). *See also* **synthetic language**. [36]

apparent-time analysis A sociolinguistic method to infer from the variable linguistic situation at a given point in time the possible future development of a feature. *See also* **real-time analysis**. [75]

assimilation The process whereby two neighbouring sounds become more similar ('partial ~') or identical ('complete ~'). [49]

back-formation The process of **word-formation** whereby a new word is coined by cutting off an imagined suffix from an existing word, owing to the morphological reinterpretation of the latter (e.g. *editor > edit*). [29]

borrowing The process of introducing a linguistic feature, especially a word or a grammatical feature, from another language or variety. [25]

chain shift A series of interrelated **unconditioned sound changes**, in which the phonetic realization of certain phonemes changes systematically, with one change initiating another, e.g. the English Great Vowel Shift. [52]

codification The process of providing a systematic description of a language in grammars and dictionaries, frequently connected with the establishment of prescriptive rules of correct usage. [6]

cognates Words or **morphemes** in **genetically related** languages which derive from a common source in the **proto-language**. [17]

comparative reconstruction The reconstruction of the non-attested **proto-language** through the systematic comparison of **cognates** in the daughter languages. [9]

compensatory lengthening The process of lengthening a sound, typically a vowel, due to the loss of a following sound. [50]

compounding The process of **word-formation** in which two independent words or 'free **morphemes**' are combined to form a new word, e.g. *letter-box* (< *letter* + *box*). [26]

conditioned sound change A sound change that occurs in specific phonetic environments. [48]

constraint A general restriction on possible linguistic changes. [76]

convergence The process whereby languages become structurally more similar to each other (as opposed to divergence, whereby they become less similar). [58]

conversion (also 'zero derivation') The **word-formation** process whereby a word changes its class, i.e. undergoes a functional shift, without formal change, such as verb to noun (*to cheat > a cheat*), or adjective or adverb to verb (*to lower, to up*). [28]

creole A **pidgin** adopted by a speech community as its first language, which develops in grammatical and lexical complexity to account for the new communicative functions. [59]

creolization The process whereby a **pidgin** elaborates its simple linguistic structures and stylistic range. [60]

decreolization The process whereby a **creole** becomes more similar to a dominant or standard language, leading to a post-creole continuum of varieties. [62]

deletion The diachronic process of omitting a linguistic element, especially a sound. [48]

devoicing The loss of voicing, i.e. the feature [voiced], as in the change from [b] > [p]. [22]

diachronic The term referring to (the study of) linguistic change over time. *See also* **synchronic**. [8]

diphthongization The change of a pure vowel into a diphthong, i.e. a vowel ending in a glide, as in [uː] > [aʊ].[47]

dissimilation The process whereby a sound becomes less similar to another, neighbouring one, as in *pilgrim* (< Latin *peregrinus*). [49]

extension of meaning The process whereby the meaning of a word becomes more general, such as Middle English *bird* 'young bird' > 'bird'. [30]

family tree A model which represents the genetic relationship of languages in the form of a tree diagram. [16]

functional load The frequency with which a phonemic opposition is used for distinguishing words or **morphemes**, such as /r/ vs. /l/ as in *read* vs. *lead*. [69]

genetically related Languages which go back to the same parent or **proto-language** are genetically related. [15]

grammaticalization The process whereby an independent lexical word gradually acquires a grammatical function, sometimes even becoming an affix, such as Latin *mens*, *mentis* 'sense' > French suffix -*ment*, as in *heureusement* 'fortunately'. [30, 39]

hypercorrection The adjustment of speech to a more prestigious norm, which results in the overuse of a linguistic feature. [74]

implementation The spread of a change in the linguistic system of individuals and/or a speech community. [77]

inflecting language A language in which grammatical relationships like number, tense, etc. are predominantly expressed by grammatical affixes. *See also* **agglutinating language**, **isolating language**. [35]

internal reconstruction A procedure whereby unattested stages of a language are reconstructed by using available material from this same language. [21]

isolate A language with no known genetical relationship to other languages, e.g. Basque. [23]

isolating language A language in which words generally consist of single and clearly distinguishable **morphemes**. *See also* **agglutinating language**, **inflecting language**. [35]

language family A group of **genetically related** languages, i.e. of languages that descend from a common **proto-language**. [16]

language planning The process of deliberate interference with the status of a language ('status ~') or aspects of its form and functions ('corpus ~'). [84]

lenition The cover term for processes which involve some 'weakening' of sounds, such as voicing, **spirantization**, vocalization of consonants, or **deletion**. [48]

lexical diffusion The gradual spread of a (sound) change through the vocabulary of a language. [78]

lingua franca A general language of communication used by people with different first languages. [61]

linguistic area A number of languages in contact within a specific geographical area, which share certain linguistic features. [58]

linguistic variable A linguistic unit for which there are alternative realizations, according to factors such as social class, age, and sex. [73]

loan word A word borrowed from another language or variety [25]

merger *see* **phonemic merger**

metaphor The transfer of a term because of a real or imagined similarity, e.g. *neck* 'part of the body' > 'part of a bottle'. [30]

metonymy The **semantic change** in which an attribute of a thing is used to denote the whole, e.g. *White House* for the American president. [30]

monophthongization The process whereby a diphthong becomes a monophthong, i.e. a vowel with a perceived stable quality, e.g. [aɪ] > [aː]. [47]

morpheme The smallest meaningful unit of language; 'free' morphemes may occur on their own, such as *cat*, while 'bound' morphemes only occur in combination with other morphemes, such as *dis-*, *-able*, etc. [22]

narrowing of meaning The meaning change in which a word becomes more specific, like *fowl* 'bird' > 'fowl'. [30]

palatalization A sound change in which the position of the tongue is fronted towards the hard palate, e.g. [u] > [y] (as in French *une*), or [k] > [ʧ] (cf. Latin *centum* [k] and Italian *cento* [ʧ] '100') . [47]

pejoration of meaning The process whereby a word loses its neutral or positive meaning and acquires a negative one, e.g. *knave* (originally 'boy'). *See also* **amelioration of meaning**. [31]

phoneme The abstract distinctive sound unit of a particular language. [45]

phonemic change A sound change on the level of the abstract phonemic system, as opposed to **phonetic change**, a change on the concrete level of speech production. [45]

phonemic merger The **phonemic change** whereby one **phoneme** merges (completely or partially) with another one, thus leading to a loss of phonemic opposition. [51]

phonemic split The **phonemic change** whereby one **phoneme** splits into two different ones; often combined with **phonemic merger**. [51]

phonetic change *see* **phonemic change**

phonological change (also **sound change**) The cover term for **phonetic change** and **phonemic change**. Some linguists, however, use the term synonymously with **phonemic change**. [45]

pidgin An auxiliary language of communication between speakers of mutually unintelligible languages, with a reduced grammatical structure, lexicon, and range of styles. [59]

proto-language The unattested common ancestor of a language family or group of languages, reconstructed by **comparative reconstruction**. [15]

real-time analysis The analysis of particular linguistic features in the same speech community at different points in time. *See also* **apparent-time analysis**. [75]

reanalysis The reinterpretation of a sequence of **morphemes** ('morphological ~') or a syntactic construction ('syntactic ~'), by reassigning them a new function or internal structure. [29, 40]

regularity hypothesis (also 'Neogrammarian hypothesis') The view that sound change is regular and without exception. [78]

relative chronology The relative temporal order in which different changes take place. [23]

relexification The extensive replacement of the vocabulary of a language by **borrowing** from another language, especially in **pidgins** and **creoles**. [60]

semantic change A change in the meaning of words or **morphemes**. [26]

spirantization The sound change from stop to fricative, as in [p] > [f]. [47]

substratum (also **substrate**) The linguistic influence of a sub-ordinate language, often given up by its original speakers, on the socially dominant adopted language. [65]

synchronic The term referring to (the study of) the state of a language at a given time, not necessarily the present. *See also* **diachronic**. [8]

synthetic language The cover term for **agglutinating** and **inflecting** languages. [36]

typology The classification of languages according to structural features (phonology, morphology, syntax). [35]

unconditioned sound change A sound change that affects all occurrences of a specific sound, irrespective of context. [48]

variable *see* **linguistic variable**

variant One of a number of possible alternative realizations of a linguistic item. [73]

velarization The sound change in which the back of the tongue is moved backwards towards the velum, e.g. [e] > [o]. [47]

word-formation The process of coining new, complex words out of existing words or **morphemes**. [25]

Acknowledgements

The author and publisher are grateful to the following for permission to reproduce extracts from copyright material:

Arnold for permission to reproduce an extract from *Historical Linguistics* by Robert L. Trask (1996).

Blackwell for permission to reproduce extracts from *Linguistic Variation and Change: On the Historical Sociolinguistics of English* by James Milroy (1992); *An Introduction to Sociolinguistics* (3rd edn.) by Ronald Wardhaugh (1998).

Cambridge University Press for permission to reproduce extracts from *Historical Linguistics and Language Change* by Roger Lass (1997); *Grammaticalization* by Paul J. Hopper and Elizabeth Closs Traugott (1993); *Historical Syntax in Cross-Linguistic Perspective* by Alice C. Harris and Lyle Campbell (1995).

Edinburgh University Press for permission to reproduce extracts from *Historical Linguistics* by Lyle Campbell (1998).

Macmillan for permission to reproduce an extract from *Contact Languages: Pidgin and Creoles* by Mark Sebba (1997).

MIT Press for permission to reproduce an extract from *Principles and Methods for Historical Linguistics* by Robert J. Jeffers and Ilse Lehiste (1979).

Mouton de Gruyter for permission to reproduce an extract from *Language History, Language Change, and Language Relationship: An Introduction to Historical and Comparative Linguistics* by Hans Henrich Hock and Brian D. Joseph (1996); 'Syntactic change and borrowing: the case of the accusative-and-infinitive construction in English' by Olga Fischer in Marinel Gerritsen and Dieter Stein (eds): *Internal and External Factors in Syntactic Change* (1992).

Oxford University Press for permission to reproduce extracts from *Linguistic Reconstruction: An Introduction to Theory and Method* by Anthony Fox (1995); *An Introduction to Historical Linguistics* (3rd edn.) by Terry Crowley (1997).

Pearson Education for permission to reproduce an extract from *An Introduction to Sociolinguistics* by Janet Holmes (Longman 1992).

Penguin Press for permission to reproduce an extract from *The Symbolic Species: The Co-Evolution of Language and the Human Brain* by Terrence Deacon (Allen Lane, Penguin Press 1997) Copyright © Terrence W. Deacon, 1997.

Routledge for permission to reproduce extracts from *Authority in Language: Investigating Standard English* (3rd edn.) by James Milroy and Lesley Milroy (1999); *On Language change: The Invisible Hand in Language* by Rudi Keller (1994); *Historical Linguistics: An Introduction* (3rd edn.) by Winfred P. Lehmann (1992).

Although every effort has been made to trace and contact copyright holders before publication, this has not always been possible. We apologize for any infringement of copyright, and if notified, the publisher will be pleased to rectify any errors or omissions at the earliest opportunity.